OCS Study
MMS 2001-013

Coastal Marine Institute

Forecasting the Number of Offshore Platforms on the Gulf of Mexico OCS to the Year 2023

I0439648

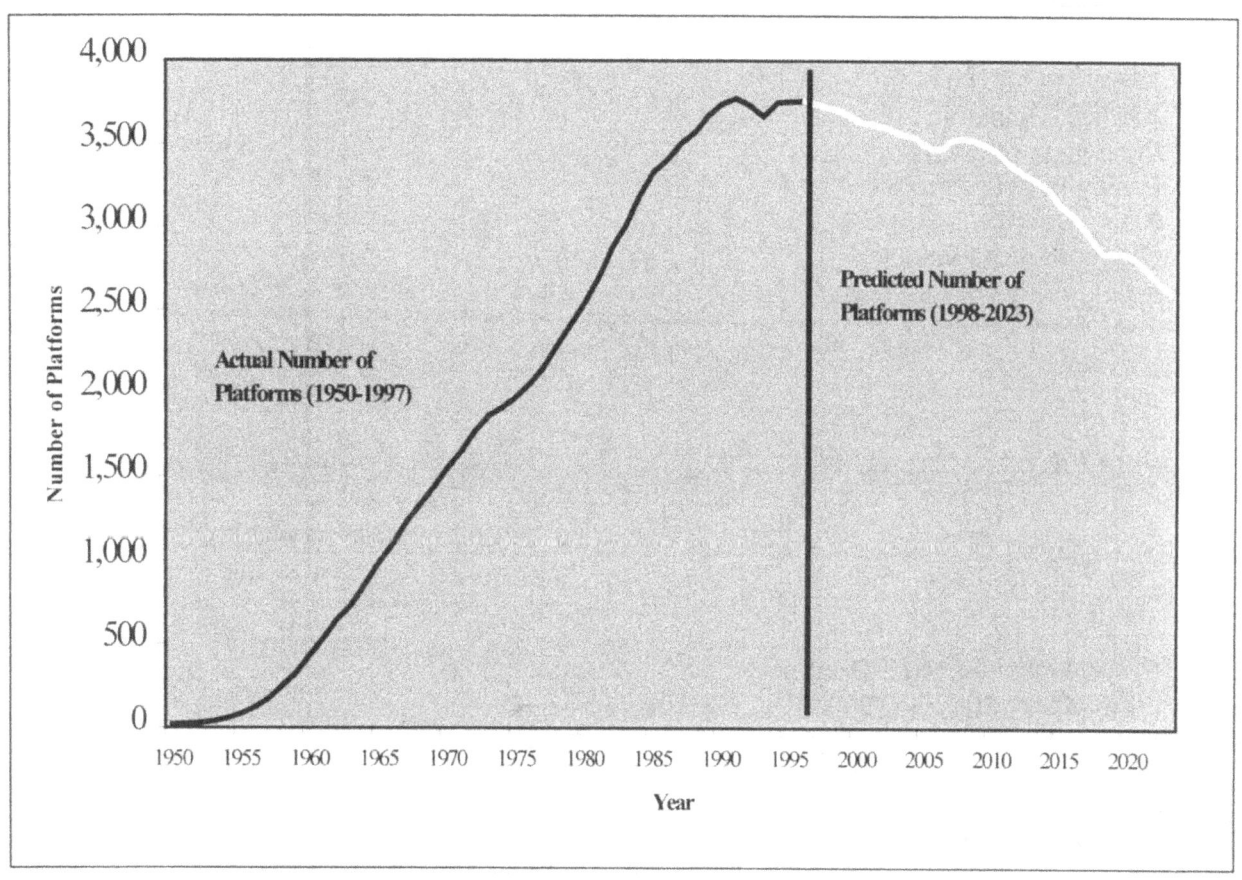

Actual Number of Platforms (1950-1997)

Predicted Number of Platforms (1998-2023)

Number of Platforms

Year

U.S. Department of the Interior
Minerals Management Service
Gulf of Mexico OCS Region

Cooperative Agreement
Coastal Marine Institute
Louisiana State University

OCS Study
MMS 2001-013

Coastal Marine Institute

Forecasting the Number of Offshore Platforms on the Gulf of Mexico OCS to the Year 2023

Authors

Allan G. Pulsipher
Omowumi O. Iledare
Dmitry V. Mesyanzhinov
Alan Dupont
Qiaozhen Lucy Zhu

April 2001

Prepared under MMS Contract
14-35-0001-30660-19934
by
Center for Energy Studies
Louisiana State University
Baton Rouge, Louisiana 70801

Published by

U.S. Department of the Interior
Minerals Management Service
Gulf of Mexico OCS Region

Cooperative Agreement
Coastal Marine Institute
Louisiana State University

DISCLAIMER

This report was prepared under contract between the Minerals Management Service (MMS) and Louisiana State University's Center for Energy Studies. This report has been technically reviewed by MMS. Approval does not signify that the contents necessarily reflect the view and policies of the Service, nor does mention of trade names or commercial products constitute endorsement or recommendation for use. It is, however, exempt from review and compliance with MMS editorial standards.

REPORT AVAILABILITY

Extra copies of the report may be obtained from the Public Information Office (Mail Stop 5034) at the following address:

U.S. Department of the Interior
Minerals Management Service
Gulf of Mexico OCS Region
Public Information Office (MS 5034)
1201 Elmwood Park Boulevard
New Orleans, Louisiana 70123-2394
Telephone Number: 1-800-200-GULF

CITATION

Suggested Citation:

Pulsipher, A.G., O.O. Iledare, D.V. Mesyanzhinov, A. Dupont, and Q.L. Zhu. 2001. Forecasting the number of offshore platforms on the Gulf of Mexico OCS to the year 2023. Prepared by the Center for Energy Studies, Louisiana State University, Baton Rouge, La. OCS Study MMS 2001-013. U.S. Department of the Interior, Minerals Management Service, Gulf of Mexico OCS Region, New Orleans, La. 52 pp.

ACKNOWLEDGMENTS

This report is based primarily on OCS drilling records made available to the Center for Energy Studies by the Minerals Management Service, New Orleans. Barbara Kavanaugh, Versa Stickle, Ric Pincomb, and William Daniel IV were very helpful in obtaining these data.

iii

ABSTRACT

The most likely, or reference, forecast of the number of operating offshore structures on the Gulf of Mexico shows a decline of about 29 percent over the period 1999 to 2023. The decline will occur because the number of platforms being removed is predicted to increase significantly above current levels, while the number of platforms being installed is predicted to increase only slightly above current levels. As a consequence of this pattern, and the larger size of the platforms being installed, overall activity in removing and installing platforms increases significantly, despite the decline in the number of operating platforms during the forecast period.

The model results on which this forecast was based explain nearly 80 percent of the variation in the historical values of the principal dependent variable–new offshore structures– and track very closely the historical trend of platform installations. The forecasts were made by using econometric modeling techniques on historical data from 1947 through 1996.

Alternative forecasts made by changing the values of the forecasting variables did not result in major differences from the reference forecast. Even spreading the range of the values used in the forecasting equations by adding two standard errors to forecasting variables did not reverse the trends in the reference forecast. Adding or subtracting two standard errors to the cumulative size of new oil and gas field developed in the Gulf and to the Energy Information Agency's forecast of oil prices resulted in forecasts in which the decline in operating platforms in high forecast was still more than 20 percent, as compared to 29 percent in the reference forecast. The decline in the corresponding low forecast was about 35 percent.

A cooperative project with MMS to extend the analysis to water depth and location has been approved and is underway under the LSU-MMS Coastal Marine Institute program.

TABLE OF CONTENTS

LIST OF FIGURES

LIST OF TABLES

EXECUTIVE SUMMARY

The forecasts in this report predict the number of new offshore structures to be installed, removed, and operated on the Gulf of Mexico OCS over the next twenty-five years–1999 to 2023. The forecasts were made by using econometric modeling techniques on historical data from 1947 through 1996. The historical record and predicted path (under the reference forecast) of the number of platforms operating in the Gulf over the 1947 to 2023 time period are illustrated in Figure E.1.

The principal trends and implications of the reference forecast are:

- A decline in the number of operating offshore structures from 3,687 to 2,612: a decline of about 29 percent over the 1999 to 2023 period.

- An annual average rate for installation of new platforms of not quite 142 per year: a total of 3,543 platforms installed over the 25-year period.

- Removal of old platforms at an annual rate of about 186 per year: a total of 4,645 structures removed over the period.

The model results on which this forecast were based explain nearly 80 percent of the variation in the historical values of the principal dependent variable–new offshore structures–and tracks very closely the historical trend in platform installations. Alternative forecasts, based on changing the values of the forecasting variables, did not result in major changes in the trends in the reference forecast.

- Using the high oil price forecast, rather than the base oil price forecast, in the forecasting model resulted in a 2.3 percent increase in the number of platforms operating in the year 2023 compared to the number in the reference forecast. The percentage decline in operating platforms over the 1999 to 2023 period decreased from 29 percent to 27 percent. In EIA's low price case, the decline in platforms deepened to a 31 percent drop.

- If the forecasting variable reflecting the cumulative size of new oil and gas fields is increased by two standard errors, the number of platforms operating in the year 2023 is forecast to increase by 16 platforms, an increase of only 0.6 percent.

- Spreading the range of the values used for both the cumulative size of new oil and gas fields discovered and for the Energy Information Administration's forecast of oil prices had a larger but still modest impact. The high forecast (based on both oil prices and the cumulative size of new fields increased by two standard errors) predicted the number of operating platforms would decline by slightly more than 20 percent, as compared to 29 percent in the reference forecast. The decline in the corresponding low forecast was about 35 percent.

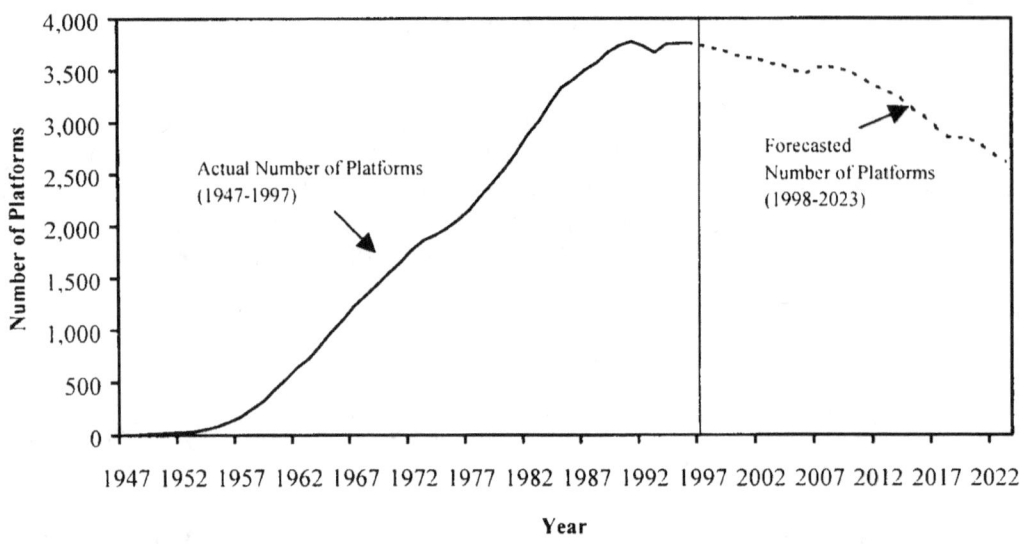

Figure E.1. Platforms operating on the Gulf of Mexico OCS.

A numerical forecast of offshore structures is relevant and useful for various purposes. For example, an important aspect of offshore platforms in the Gulf of Mexico is that they provide habitat for highly valued reef fish such as snappers and groupers. Such habitat is scarce in the Gulf. Offshore platforms have increased the total amount of reef habitat available by as much as 10 to 25 percent, depending on the definition and estimate of natural reef habitat, and have become important destinations for recreational fishermen and party boats. A forecast of the number of platforms operating over the next twenty-five years will be useful to those responsible for planning, managing, and preserving fish habitat and fish stocks through artificial reefs and other management programs.

The internal content and mechanics of the forecast also are important. For example, the economies of coastal areas adjacent to offshore petroleum producing areas are affected in important ways by offshore oil or gas development. In the reference forecast the decline in the number of operating platforms takes place because the number of platforms removed each year increases significantly above historical levels. The annual number of platforms installed, on the other hand, increases as well, but very slowly.

Since many of the platforms installed are expected to be larger platforms located in deeper water further from shore while more of the platforms forecast to be removed are smaller platforms located in shallower waters, expenditures on installing and operating new platforms and pipelines (as well as on removing old platforms) will dwarf expenditures lost as smaller platforms cease operating. Thus, the net effect on the economies of adjacent coastal areas may be quite positive despite the overall decline in the number of platforms operating. In contrast, if the same decline in the operating platforms as in the reference forecast were to come about largely

2

because of a decline in the number of platforms installed, with a more modest decline relative to the reference forecast in the number of platforms removed, such a decline would likely have a very significant negative effect on adjacent coastal areas.

The report also reviewed the history of offshore development as a background and context for the forecast. The principal findings and generalizations from this review are:

- Since 1942, 5,561 platforms or structures have been installed on the OCS subject to federal jurisdiction.

- As of 1997, 1,645 of these structures had been removed leaving 3,916 operating platforms on the federal OCS.

- About 50 percent of the operating platforms are classified as "non-major" structures–defined as having fewer than six wells and no more than two pieces of equipment. The other 50 percent are classified as "major structures."

- About 68 percent of the structures that have been removed were non-major structures, and about 86 percent of the structures that have been removed were located in less than 400 feet of water.

- Conversely, proportionately more larger platforms, located in deeper water, have been installed as time has passed.

- The number of operating structures has grown steadily since the initial installations in the 1940s because the number of installations has been greater than the number of removals.

- The growth of the number of operating platforms has slowed in the 1990s as yields from fields have declined and the platforms installed in the 1960s and 1970s to produce them have become uneconomic to operate and have been removed.

- The average age of operating platforms has steadily increased; in 1997 it was about 18 years for major structures and 16 years for non-major structures.

- The average age of platforms that have been removed was 14.5 years for major structures and 15.8 years for non-major structures.

- Many external factors are involved in the decision to install a platform, but the determining factor is the expected productivity and profitability of the field the platform is intended to produce. When production falls below profitable levels, the platform will be shut down and removed.

- When new fields are discovered, new structures will be installed if expected revenues exceed expected costs sufficiently to compensate the operator for the risk, uncertainty, and opportunity cost of capital inherent in the installation decision. Factors that increase

3

expected revenues or decrease uncertainty and risk will accelerate installations; factors having the opposite effects will decrease installations.

- The decision to remove a platform is more tightly constrained. Economic and cash flow considerations may influence the timing of decisions at the margin, but regulations require structures to be removed within one year after production on the lease has stopped. Structures may be removed before that time if economic or technical factors so dictate, and operators may ask that removal be postponed, but the range of managerial discretion is much narrower than it is for installations.

* * * * *

1. INTRODUCTION

There have been about 5,600 offshore structures installed and operated by oil and gas companies in the United States.[1] Most of them are located in the Gulf of Mexico off the coasts of Louisiana and Texas, with small clusters also off Alabama, Alaska, California, and Mississippi. The structures range in size from single-well caissons in shallow water to huge, complex structures located in very deep water that would dwarf the tallest existing skyscrapers were they to be located on dry land. These varied structures are usually lumped together as "offshore platforms" or, even less descriptively, called "oil rigs," but they at the extreme they are as different as lawnmowers and jet airplanes.

The nation's stock of offshore platforms is one of the primary components of its economic and physical capital. Constructing, operating, and removing platforms interacts with the economies and ecologies of adjacent coastal areas in important ways (positively as well as negatively). Although firms operating in the Gulf of Mexico conduct detailed engineering and economic planning studies to schedule platform installations and removals on their leases, little analysis has focused on how the entire collection of offshore platforms is likely to change over time and what variables or influences are responsible for those changes.

The objectives of this study are as follows:

- First, to make a forecast of the number of offshore platforms that will be removed, installed, and operated in the Gulf over the next two decades, and

- Second, to discuss the principal determinants and characteristics of the forecast as well as some of the uncertainties and implications of this forecast for the industries and individuals that use the Gulf's resources and the agencies that are responsible for their management and regulation.

The econometric framework developed in this study assumes that as more new fields are discovered and developed, the incentives to install new offshore structures should also increase, but, at a decreasing rate. Bearing in mind the relatively long lead time required to design, permit, and install an offshore platform, however, it is likely that the strengthened incentives may not result in a platform being fully installed and operating during the given year. Other factors such as changes in economic conditions and expectations or cost-reducing- improvements in technologies will also affect the number of platforms and the rate that firms wish to install them. As economic conditions and expectations become more favorable and stable, the incentives to install new offshore structures will strengthen. Similarly, as technologies for finding and producing petroleum improve, the need for additional offshore structures may change.

---

[1]   The definition of "platform" varies. A major source of offshore data, for example, does not include single pipe caissons or well protectors while the Minerals Management Service does include such structures in their data. We will rely on MMS data definitions unless noted otherwise.

Technological change is often divided into two broad categories: 1) evolutionary technological change– the steady refinement of techniques and equipment, and 2) revolutionary technological change– the sudden, sharp change brought about by completely new techniques and equipment. The first is always present to some degree as firms and their employees gain experience, but the second is by definition difficult if not impossible to predict and incorporate into long-term forecasts.

Does this limit the relevance of our forecast? Would the movement of drilling and production platforms into the "deep gulf" have occurred without the development of 3D seismic, directional drilling and the development of deep water technologies? Are these technologies "revolutionary" or are they "evolutionary." Does a forecast based on historical data implicitly give too little weight to these "new" technologies?

Doug Bohi (1997), in a careful consideration of the role of sources of innovation and productivity improvement in petroleum exploration and development, provides a justification for treating the emergence of these technologies as "evolutionary." Bohi writes:

> It would be a mistake to underestimate the extent to which endogenous influences were responsible for the development of these technologies. None of them suddenly appeared in the last ten years in readily usable commercial form. In fact, all three technologies are better described as groups of complementary technologies that support a central concept. Thus, for example, high-speed computers were the essential breakthrough necessary to implement the concept of 3D, but this event by itself was not sufficient for success. Computers had to be told how to process the data, and methods had to be developed for understanding what the processed data meant (Bohi. 1997, p. 101).

Bohi also explains that, although these technologies have greatly reduced finding and production costs for petroleum in the Gulf of Mexico, their impact in regions of the world where finding costs are already very low, such as the Middle East, or where transportation costs dominate, such as in the several countries of the former Soviet Union, will be small.

This report has five sections. An introduction, a second section presenting some historical trends, a third section explaining the modeling framework adopted in this report, a fourth section describing the hypothesized model equations and presenting the estimated model results, and a final section summarizing findings, implications and conclusions.

2. THE NUMBER OF OFFSHORE PLATFORMS ON THE GULF OCS

2.1 Installations

Since the first offshore structure was located in the OCS Gulf in 1942, 5,561 fixed structures[2] had been installed as of December 31, 1997. Over the same time period about 1,645 platforms had been removed leaving about 3,916 fixed structures that are currently operating. Approximately 77 percent of platforms were installed in water depth of less than 150 feet. In aggregate since 1942, 53 percent of fixed offshore structures installed on the OCS were non-major offshore structures. Thus, 47 percent of all OCS structures installed since 1942 are major oil and gas drilling and production platforms. The number of platforms installed annually on the OCS averaged about 101 between 1942 and 1997.

Data on the number of fixed offshore structures installed in the Gulf of Mexico OCS region are presented in Table 2.1 both by water depth and type of structure. Structures are classified as either major or non-major. Structures with at least six completions and two pieces of production equipment are major structures; all others are classified as non-major.

Table 2.1

Number of Offshore Structures Installed by Water Depth and Type: Gulf OCS as of December 31, 1997

Depth Ranges	Major Structures	Non-Major Structures	All Structures
0 - 20	103	512	615
21-50	523	1,427	1,950
51-100	698	774	1,472
101-150	393	176	569
151-200	311	107	418
201-300	338	48	386
301-400	86	7	93
401-500	22	0	22
501-900	18	2	20
> 900	14	2	16
Total	2,506	3,055	5,561

---

[2]   There are an additional 272 structures in the MMS data file. However, these are not included in the analysis because no installation date is indicated for these structures.

Figure 2.1 shows the number of platforms installed on the Gulf of Mexico OCS during the 1942 to 1997 period.[3] Only a weak, positive, pattern of growth is observable, especially if the price spike in the early 1980s is not considered to be a part of the longer-term trend and the initial ramp-up in the 1950s is omitted. The initiation of area-wide leasing in 1983 is another factor that appears to have influenced the trend in installations.

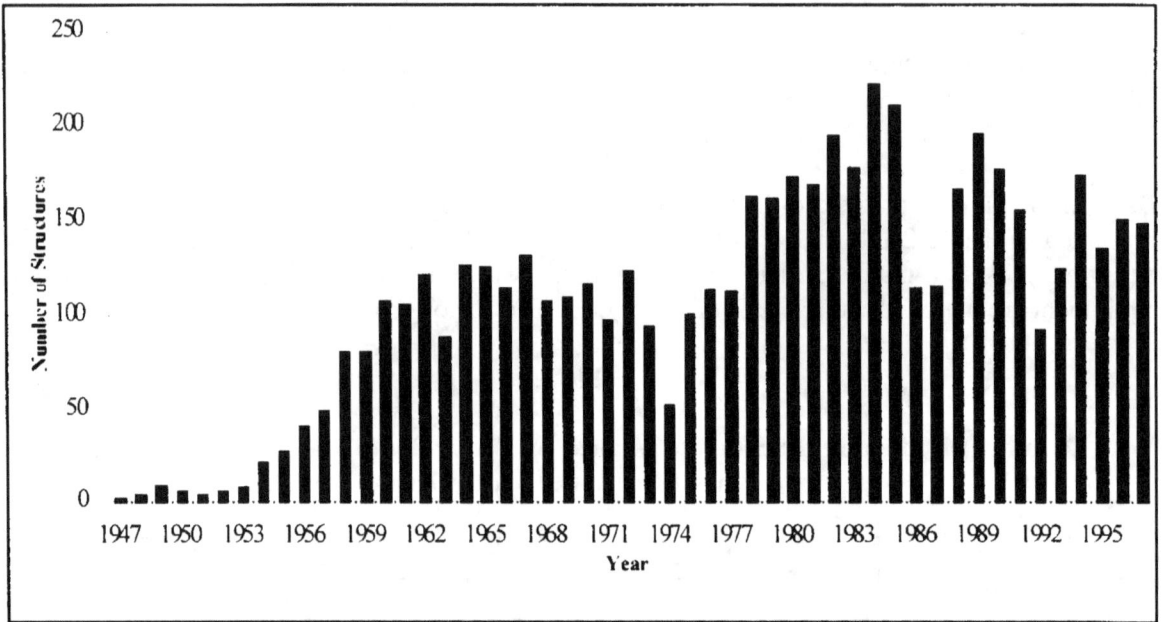

Figure 2.1. Fixed offshore structures installed on the OCS, 1947-1997.

2.2 Removals

Standard industry practice is to remove platforms at the end of the economic life of the field in which they are located. Their removal thus, to a large extent, depends directly on the duration of oil and gas production from the lease on which they are located. Although other factors may come into play, usually it is less expensive to remove several or all the platforms in a field at the same time rather than to remove each when its own production falls below minimum levels of profitability. Thus, platforms normally will not be removed before production from the lease on which they are located comes to an end.

Further, since earlier removal is not required by existing regulations, companies may choose to postpone removals simply because doing so may reduce the discounted (or present value) future cost of doing so below the current cost of removal. Other reasons for early removal or

---

[3]   Although the first platform on the OCS was installed in 1942, consecutive time-series data on platform installations began in 1947.

postponing removal include damage to the platform, services performed for other platforms such as pumping or processing, or planning or considering work overs or drilling at a new depth.

According to available data on platform removals, the first offshore structure was removed from the Gulf of Mexico OCS in 1973. To date (through 1997), 1,645 structures have been removed at an annual average rate of 65 removals. Figure 2.2 shows total platforms removed per year and the cumulative number of platforms removed in the Gulf of Mexico OCS region from 1973 through 1997. An unusually high number of offshore structures were removed in 1993 because of damage caused by Hurricane Andrew.

Figure 2.3 shows the average age of platforms removed by type of structure. As of year end 1997, the average age of all removed offshore structures was 14 years. When major and non-major platforms are measured separately, the average age at removal for major structures is 14.5 and 15.8 for non-major structures.

Although accidents, storm damage, and unforseen geological problems may cause platforms to be removed early, the discrepancy between the assumed and actual life of platforms is probably explained by the end of economic production from the field rather than by design or engineering factors unique to each platform.

Table 2.2 shows the average depth of the water surrounding offshore structures removed in the U.S. Gulf of Mexico OCS region as of 1997. The bulk of platforms removed (90 percent) was removed in water depth of less than 150 feet. In addition, nearly 70 percent of platforms removed as of 1997 are non-major offshore structures.

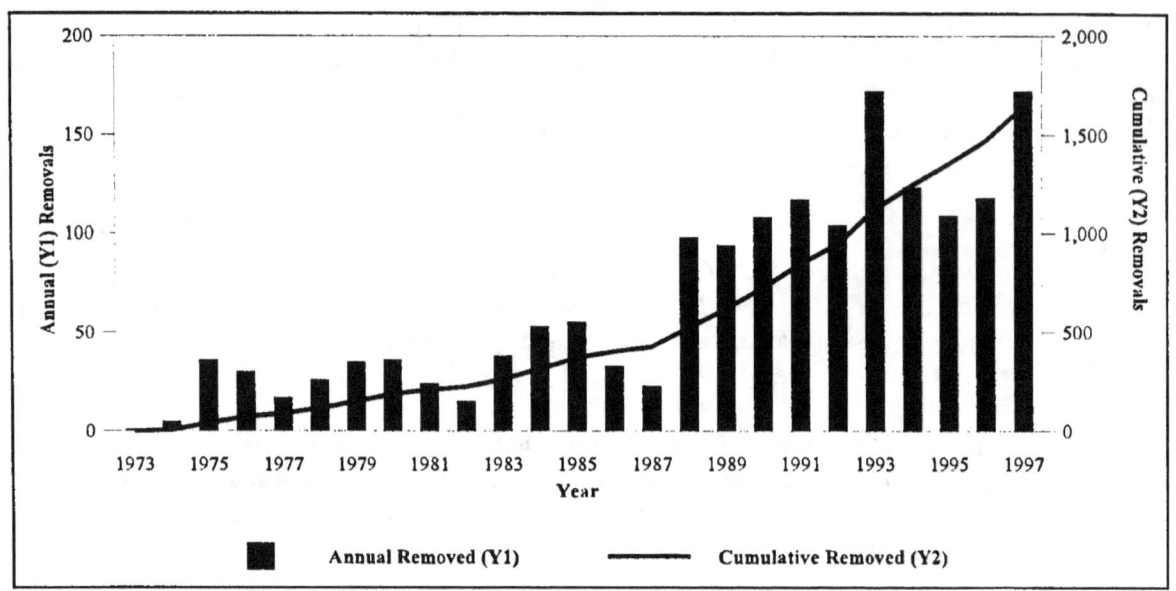

Figure 2.2. Fixed offshore structures removed on the OCS, 1973-1997.

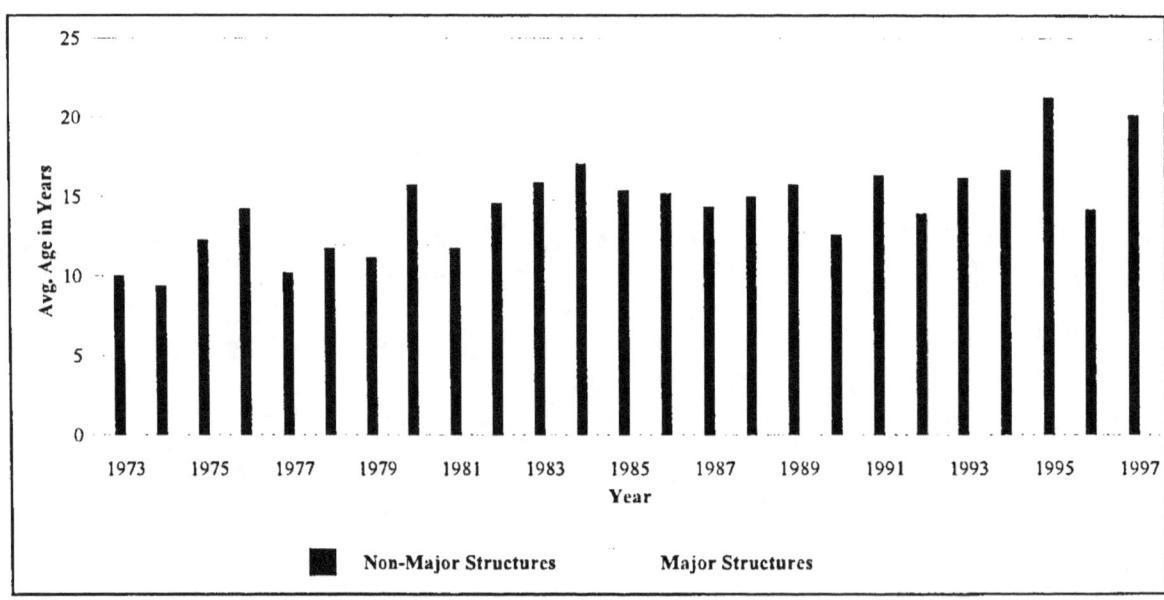

Figure 2.3. Average age of fixed offshore structures removed on the OCS, 1973-1997.

10

Table 2.2

**Water Depth of Fixed Offshore Structures Removed on the Gulf of Mexico OCS
1973-1997**

Depth Ranges	Non-Major Structures	Major Structures	All Structures
0-20	240	25	265
21-50	513	124	637
51-100	274	174	448
101-150	52	87	139
151-200	29	66	95
201-300	4	40	44
301-400	1	15	16
401-500	0	0	0
501-900	0	0	0
> 900	0	1	1
Total	1,113	532	1,645

2.3 Platforms in Operation

As of December 31, 1997, there were about 3,916 operational offshore structures located in waters regulated by the Minerals Management Service in the Gulf of Mexico. The number of existing offshore structures on the OCS is presented for the years 1947 through 1997 in Figure 2.4.

The total number of platforms grew in every year except 1992, when Hurricane Andrew blew through the heart of the Gulf of Mexico's producing area. Existing platforms classified by water depth are shown in Table 2.3. Of these, 80 percent were located in water depths of less than 150 feet and less than 1 percent located in waters deeper than 400 feet.

The average age of existing offshore structures on the OCS in 1997 was approximately 16.8 years. Major structures on average were 17.8 years old, and non-major structures were 15.9 years old. The productivity of platforms in terms of production per platform is illustrated in Figure 2.5. Production per platform, expressed in barrels of oil equivalent, peaked in the early 1970s and then, with the exception of the immediate post-Arab oil exporters' "embargo," declined regularly thereafter. The rate of decline leveled off, however, in the mid-1980s as seismic advances, directional drilling and other technological advances began to take hold. In the 1990s the decline essentially has stopped . As the large "deep Gulf" fields begin production in the late 1990s, production per platform may increase.

11

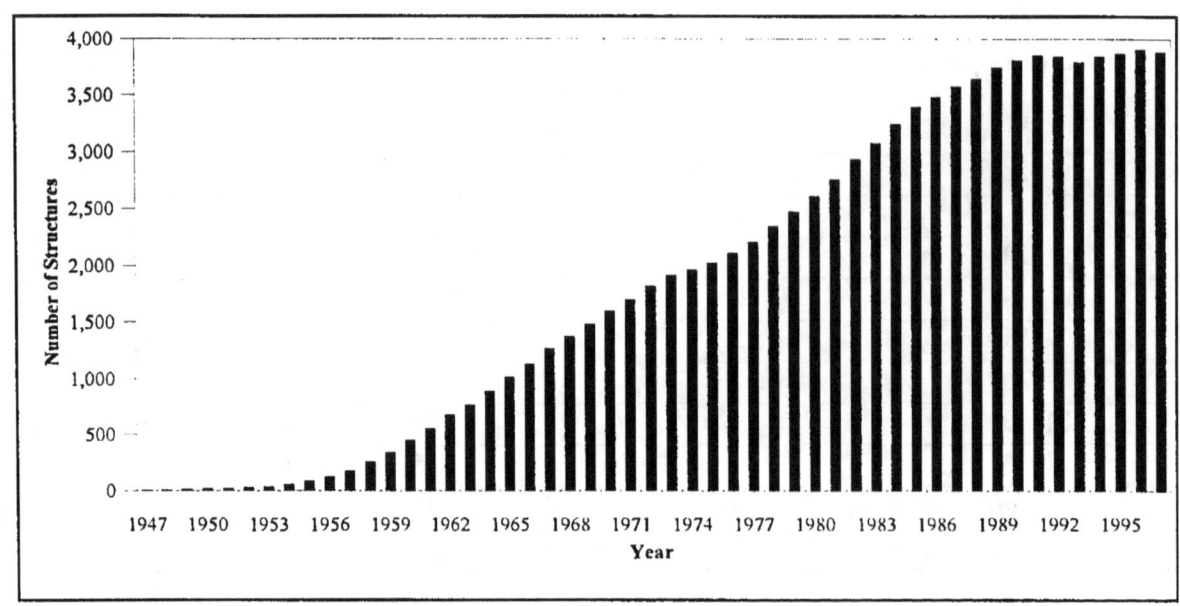

Figure 2.4. Existing offshore structures on the Gulf of Mexico OCS, 1947-1997.

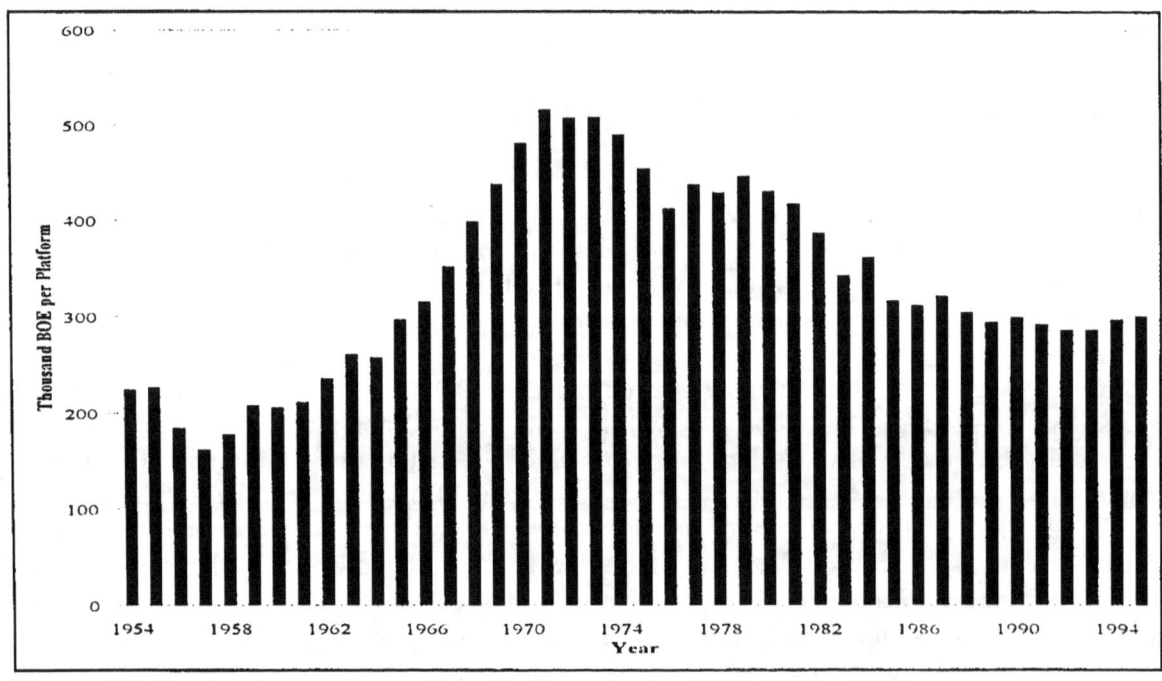

Figure 2.5. Production per operating platform on the OCS, 1954 - 1995.

Table 2.3

**Water Depth of Fixed Offshore Structures Operating on the Gulf of Mexico OCS
as of December 31, 1997**

Depth Ranges	Non-Major Structures	Major Structures	All Structures
0-20	272	78	350
21-50	914	399	1,313
51-100	500	524	1,024
101-150	124	306	430
151-200	78	245	323
201-300	44	298	342
301-400	6	71	77
401-500	0	22	22
501-900	2	18	20
> 900	2	13	15
Total	1,942	1,974	3,916

Figures 2.6 and 2.7 depict the trend in average age of major offshore structures and non-major structures on the OCS. Both figures show a steady increase, but Figure 2.6 shows apparent "leveling off" in the early 1980s followed by a resumption of the trend in the late 1980s and early 1990s. A possible explanation is that improved exploration technology and falling finding costs have made smaller fields serviced by smaller platforms profitable to develop.

This inference is consistent with the platform age data, shown in Figure 2.8, showing that about 23 percent of non-major structures on the Gulf OCS are five or fewer years old. At the other end of the distribution, approximately one-fourth of existing platforms on the OCS region are more than 25 years old, and some platforms in both the major and non-major categories are 46 years or older as depicted in Figures 2.8 and 2.9.

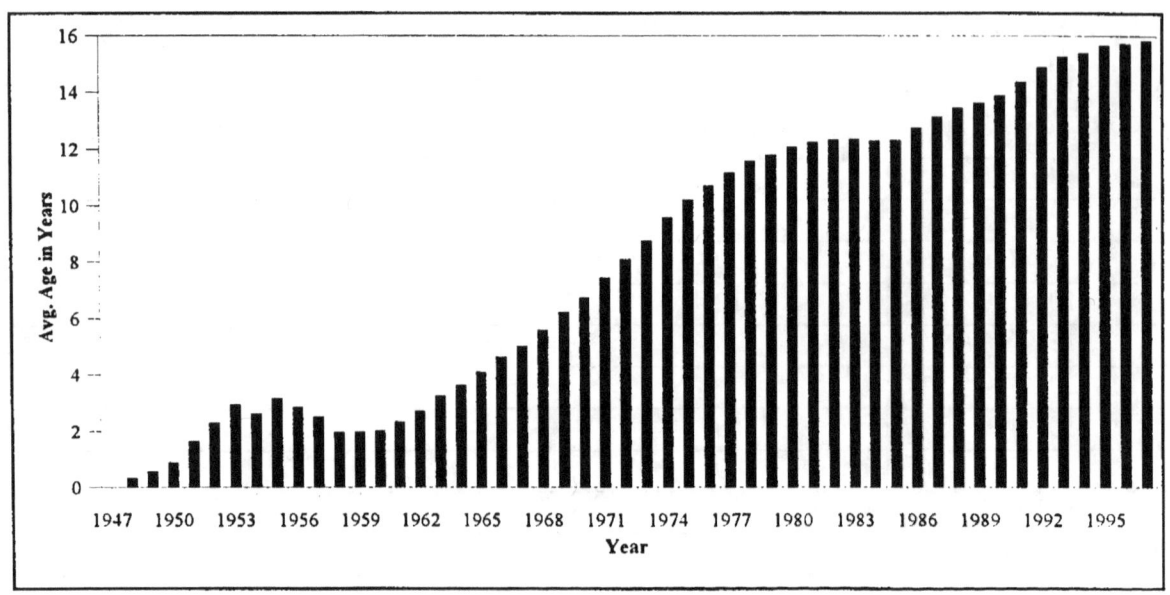

Figure 2.6. Average age of fixed non-major offshore structures operating on the OCS.

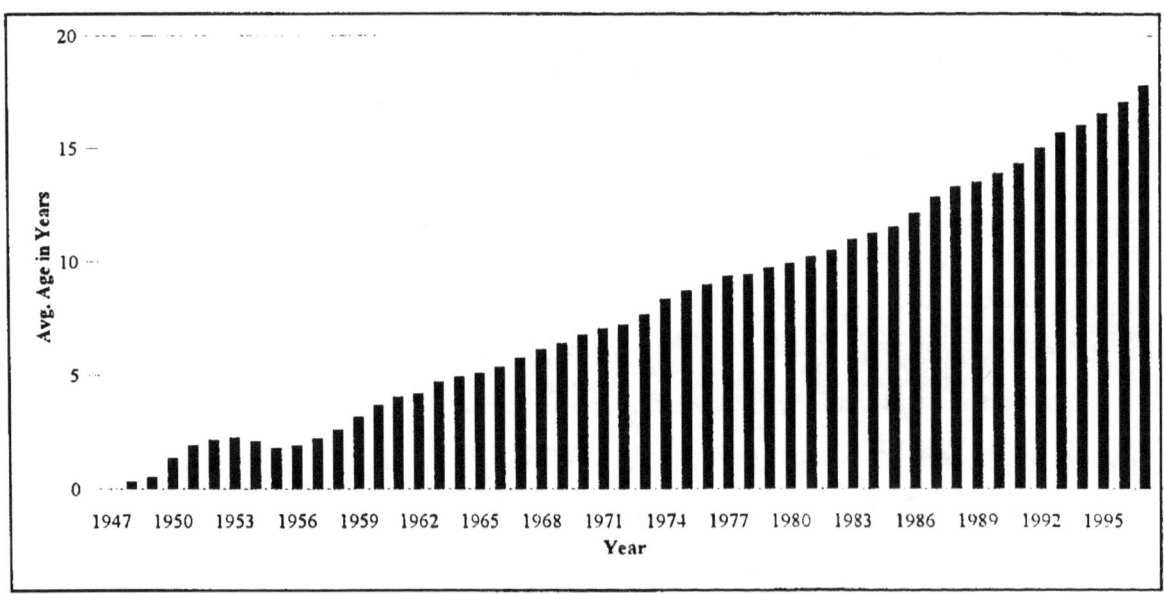

Figure 2.7. Average age of fixed major offshore structures operating on the OCS.

14

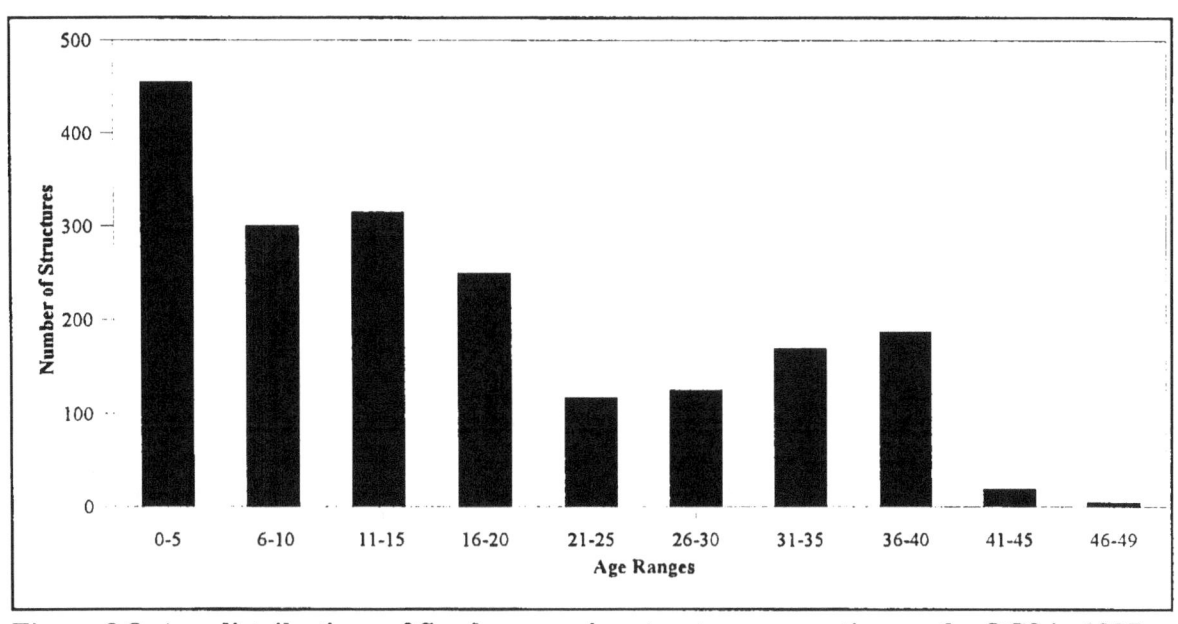

Figure 2.8. Age distributions of fixed non-major structures operating on the OCS in 1997.

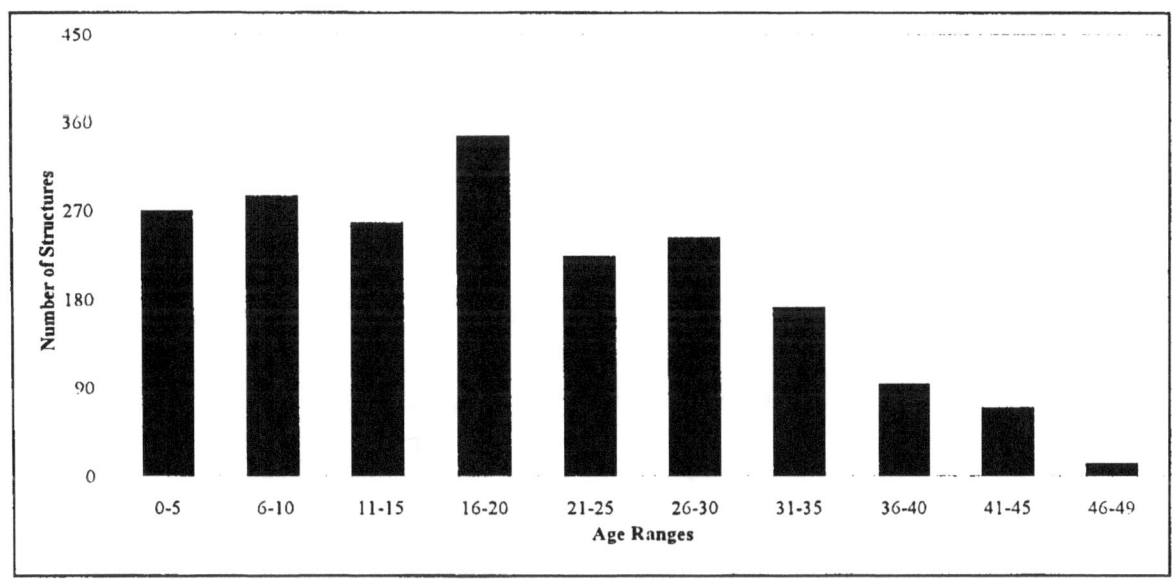

Figure 2.9. Age distribution of fixed major structures operating on the OCS in 1997.

2.4 Conclusions and Implications

- Since 1942, 5,561 platforms or structures had been installed on the OCS subject to federal jurisdiction.

- As of 1997, 1,645 of these structures had been removed leaving 3,916 operating platforms on the federal OCS.

- About 50 percent of the operating platforms are classified as "non-major" structures—defined as having fewer than six wells and no more than two pieces of equipment. The other 50 percent are classified as "major structures."

- About 68 percent of the structures that have been removed were non-major structures, and about 86 percent of the structures that have been removed were located in less than 400 feet of water

- Conversely, proportionately more larger platforms, located in deeper water, have been installed as time has passed.

- The number of operating structures has grown steadily since the initial installations in the 1940s because the number of installations has been greater than the number of removals.

- The growth of the number of operating platforms has slowed in the 1990s as platforms installed in the 1960s and 1970s have become uneconomic to operate and been removed.

- The average age of operating platforms was steadily increased and in 1997 was about 17.8 years for major structures and 15.9 years for non-major structures.

- The average age of platforms that have been removed was 14.5 years for major structures and 15.8 for non-major structures.

- Many external factors are involved in the decision to install a platform. But the determining factor is the expected productivity and profitability of the field the platform is intended to produce from. When production falls below profitable levels the platform will be shut down and removed unless other factors, such as loss of a pumping station, would increase costs sufficiently to negate the potential savings.

- When new fields are discovered, new structures will be installed if expected prices exceed expected costs sufficiently to compensate the operator for the risk, uncertainty, and opportunity cost of capital inherent in the decision. Factors that increase expected revenues or decrease uncertainty and risk will accelerate installations; factors having the opposite effects will decrease installations.

- The decision to remove a platform is more tightly constrained. Economic and cash flow considerations may influence decisions at the margin, but regulations require structures to be removed by the end of one year after production on the lease has stopped. Structures may be removed before that time if economic or technical factors so dictate, and operators may ask that removal be postponed, but the range of managerial discretion is much narrower than it is for installations.

3. MODELING THE NUMBER OF OFFSHORE PLATFORMS ON THE OCS

To forecast the number of offshore structures to be operated on the Gulf of Mexico OCS over the next two decades, we make use of the arithmetic identity that the stock of operating platforms on the OCS in a given period can be estimated as cumulative platforms installed less cumulative platforms removed.

Symbolically, the above definition translates to an identity equation of the form:

$$OPP_t = OPP_{t-1} + INS_t - REM_t \qquad (3-1)$$

where:

OPP(t) is the number of operated platforms in time t
INS(t) equals number of installed platforms in time t
REM(t) represents the number of platforms removed in time t.

The definition set forth in equation (3-1) forms the basis for the modeling approach to forecasting the number of platform installed, removed, and operated on the OCS in this report.

3.1 Model Specification

According to equation (3-1), the number of platforms operated in a given period depends on the number of platforms removed and installed during the period, *ceteris paribus*. To use this identity to forecast, we have to be able to model and forecast those factors that explain platform installations and platform removals. For the sake of simplicity it is assumed that a platform installed in a given period on the OCS becomes operational during that period. Also assumed is that the number of removed platforms in a given year is some function of the stock of operating platforms at the end of the previous year as well as the age of the platform.

The number of platforms removed in year t can be expressed the sum of the proportion of platforms installed in previous periods that were removed in the current period.

Symbolically we may represent this proposition as follows:

$$REM_t = \Sigma (\alpha_j * INS_{t-j}) \qquad (3-2)$$

where:

α_j represents the proportion of platforms removed in year t that was installed in year t-j such that $0 \le \alpha_j \le 1$ and j represents the age of removed platform.

Platforms are installed for the purpose of developing and producing discovered oil and gas reserves. As firms explore for and discover new fields they will install new platforms to produce oil or gas from them, *ceteris paribus*. This relationship would not be questioned by oil industry veterans, but skeptics might argue that the two are merely associated with a third factor that the

19

analysts has missed, or, perhaps, that the association is in some strange way the reverse of that postulated, i.e., installing platforms may cause new oil and gas fields to be found rather than the reverse.

Fortunately, an econometrician has developed statistical tests of causation, termed "Granger causality," to clarify such situations. Causality defines a condition of feedback or the presence of a feedback of one variable to another, and by implication Granger non-causality defines the absence of such a feedback. In our case, our hypothesized relationship between the discovery of new fields and the installation of platforms passes the "Granger causality" tests.[4]

However, because of short-run changes in the petroleum economy and political environment, and perhaps other determinants such as structural changes in the industry, the number of planned platforms or offshore structures to be installed in the Gulf of Mexico OCS region may not be fully accomplished in a given period.

Thus, to include such factors, the functional equation describing platform installation behavior is specified as follows:

$$INS^*_t = \beta_0 + \beta_1 \log (CFZ_t) + \beta_2 CPR_t + \beta_3 TEK_t + \beta_4 D86 + \varepsilon_t \qquad (3\text{-}3)$$

where:

β_i (i=0,1,2,3,4) are constant parameters to be estimated
INS^*_t = desired or planned number of installations in period t.
CFZ_t = cumulative total field size at the beginning of period t
CPR_t = the average current crude oil price on the Gulf OCS
TEK_t = time trend as a proxy for technical progress
D86 = dummy variable, such that, D86 = 1 for time period after 1986 and zero otherwise
ϵ_t = independent random error term

The dummy variable D86 is included to capture the effects of changes in expectations and behavior of the oil and gas industry in the Gulf of Mexico OCS subsequent to the collapse of the world crude oil market in the summer of 1986.

The short run adjustment process can be measured using the following partial adjustment model specification:

$$INS_t - INS_{t-1} = \lambda(INS^*_t - INS_{t-1}) + \omega_t \qquad (3\text{-}4)$$

---

[4] A pair-wise Granger causality test showed that cumulative field size measured in million barrels of oil equivalent does seem to Granger-cause the number of platforms installed to vary as postulated at the 90 percent significance or confidence level. The test also showed that, at nearly the 99 percent level of significance, the natural logarithm of cumulative field size does Granger-cause the number of platforms installed to vary. Having failed to reject the null hypothesis that the number of platforms does not Granger-cause either cumulative field size or the logarithm of cumulative field size, it is very plausible that past values of the logarithm of cumulative field size should be able to help predict future values of the number of platforms installed. See, Kennedy (1992)

where:

> λ represents the rate of response of the change in installed platforms to the difference between the desired installations and past value of installed platforms such that $0 \le \lambda \ge 1$, and $\omega =$ independent random error term.

Conceptually, equation (3-4) measures the proportion of adjustment to the desired number of platforms achieved within a year. The error term ω measures the failure of the adjustment process to accomplish the desired number of platforms.

Substituting equation (3-4) into equation (3-3) and simplifying the new equation yields an equation describing the relationship between the number of platforms installed (or to be installed) and its determinants.

$$INS_t = \lambda\beta_0 + \lambda\beta_1 \log(CFZ_t) + \lambda\beta_2 CPR_t + \lambda\beta_3 TEK_t + \lambda\beta_4 D86 + (1-\lambda)INS_{t-1} + \lambda\varepsilon_t + \varpi_t \qquad (3\text{-}5)$$

If $\pi_i = \lambda\beta_i$, then

$$INS_t = \pi_0 + \pi_1 \log(CFZ_t) + \pi_2 CPR_t + \pi_3 TEK_t + \pi_4 D86 + \pi_5 INS_{t-1} + \theta_t \qquad (3\text{-}6)$$

The independent or explanatory variables and their hypothesized relationships to the dependent variable, INS, are defined as follows:

> $\log(CFZ_t)$–The logarithm of cumulative field size in million barrels of oil equivalent (MMBOE). Our hypothesis is that as the size of field increases on the OCS, the number of installed platform will increase at a decreasing rate. The coefficient π_1 is expected to be positive.

> CPR_t–Current crude oil price on the Gulf of Mexico OCS. The hypothesized relationship is that the economic environment will tend to shift the long time relationship between installed platforms and cumulative discovery outwards. This means that we expect a positive coefficient for CPR, our measure of economic conditions.

> TEK_t–This is a proxy for the impact of technology on platform installations. The expectation is that the more rapid technical progress has been over the past 10-15 years the fewer the number of platforms that need to be installed to produce a given level of reserves. Less abstractly, as technologies such as horizontal and directional drilling, down-hole completion, etc., are developed, fewer platforms will be required to develop new fields in deeper water.

> D86–Dummy variables for changes in expectations and behavior since the collapse of the world oil prices are expected to affect negatively the shifting effect of prices on the relationship between platforms and discovery size.

The collapse of world crude oil prices in 1986 brought with it several organizational and institutional changes on the OCS including a massive reduction in employment, an increase in

21

the importance of independent operators, an increase in reliance on contract services, and the adoption of less hierarchical decision-making as well as technological innovations (Bohi, 1997). The likely effect of these changes on platform installation on the OCS is examined by including an interaction between the 1986 dummy variable and time trend such that the interactive dummy equals 1 from 1986 forward and 0 otherwise.

Econometric models were also estimated for platform removals, but in our view these did not result in as credible forecasts as the statistical technique used in our reference forecast. These econometric forecasts predicted near equality between installations and removals and, thus, little change in the number of operating platforms. One reason for this may have been the much shorter and more variable data series on removals compared with installations. However in our view these "constant-platform" forecasts did not seem consistent with industry trends.

3.2 Estimated Platform Installation Equation

The Ordinary Least Square (OLS) estimation results for equation (3-6) are presented in Table 3.1[5]. Equation (3-6) is a linear-log model. The general expectation from our model specification using the linear log function is that the greater the size of new fields, the larger the number of platforms to be installed, but the increase in platform installation occurs at a declining rate with cumulative size of new field additions.

Overall, the model results explain nearly 80 percent of the variation in the values of the dependent variables. The point estimate of the coefficient of the lagged value of the dependent variable is 0.463, making the adjustment coefficient 0.537. Thus we expect that firms, on average, achieve about 54 percent of their desired or planned number of platforms to be installed within a given year according to our results.

The parameter estimate for the variable representing the economic environment– the average current price of OCS crude oil– is positive as expected. Therefore, we conclude that a favorable economic environment, according to our model, leads to a statistically significant increase in the number of installed platforms. The short run price elasticity of platform installation on the OCS is estimated as 0.25; and since the adjustment coefficient is 0.537, the long-run price elasticity of platform installation by our model estimate is approximately 0.46. This means that a 10 percent increase in the current average price of OCS crude oil will lead to about 4.6 percent increase in the number of platforms installed over the long run compared to a short-run increase of about 2.5 percent.

---

[5] The data used for estimating equation (3-6) are from the MMS Gulf of Mexico OCS region in New Orleans. A Dickey-Fuller test for stationary was performed for INS, CFZ and log (CFZ) data series. The test suggests that INS and CFZ are non-stationary but log (CFZ) is stationary. It must be noted that the number of observations used for the test is relatively small. Having found that INS and CFZ are cointegrated according to our Johansen cointegration test, we estimated a cointegration and error correction model of platform installation. The results are not significantly different from those presented in Table 3.1.

The results show that cumulative field size is an important determinant of the number of platforms installed. As expected, the coefficient is positive and statistically significant at the 99 percent significant level. However, the short run and long run elasticity of cumulative reserves is on average significantly less than unity.

The empirical result is consistent with our expectation that since 1986, platform installation did decrease as a result of structural changes in the industry, deep water drilling techniques and completion technology. However, the point estimate of the interactive dummy included in the regression to capture the effects of technology and institutional changes, although negative as expected, is not statistically different from zero.

Figure 3.1 shows that the prediction using equation (3-6) presented in Table 3.1 tracks the actual trend in platform installation very closely.

Table 3.1

OLS Estimates of the Platform Installation Model (t-statistics in parenthesis)

Variable	Coefficient
Intercepts	-113.931
	(-2.847)
Cumulative New	
Fields (CFZ)	16.618
	(3.118)
Average Current	
OCS Oil Price (CPR)	2.089
	(2.416)
Number of Platform	
Installed (INS_{t-1})	0.457
	(3.641)
Technical Progress	-0.163
(Interactive Dummy)	(-0.706)

Observations	49	
Adjusted R^2	0.791	
Error of Regression	27	

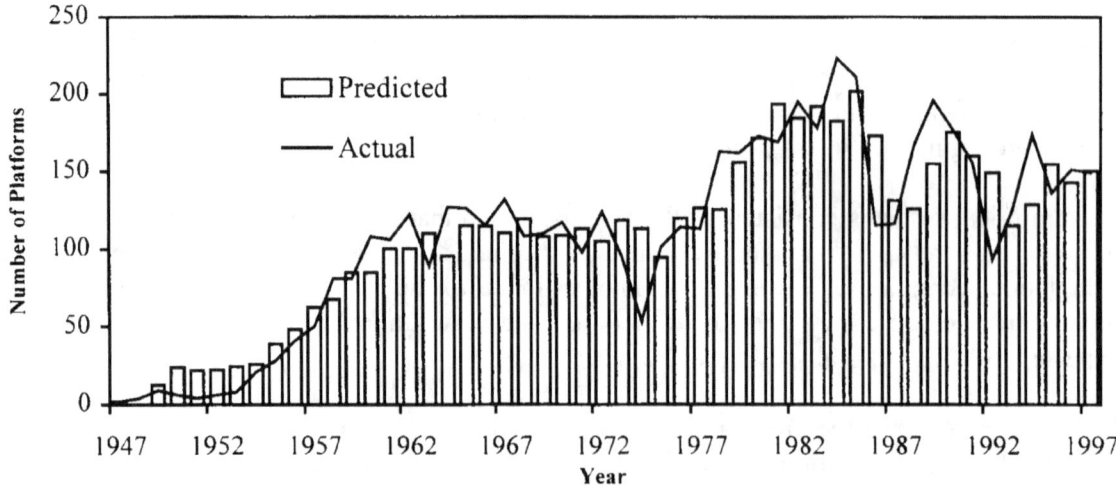

Figure 3.1. Actual and predicted number of platforms installed.

3.3 Platform Removal Equation

The statistical equation applied in this paper for predicting platform removals is a reduced form of equation (3-2) reproduced below in an estimated form as equation (3-7):

$$REM_t = 0.953 INS_{t-33} + 0.351 INS_{t-21} \tag{3-7}$$

Of the several alternative forms of equation (3-2) that we examined, equation (3-7) yields the best statistical fit to the available historical data on removed platforms.[6]

In order to model the physical reality in which only installed platforms can be removed, we selected a specification with a suppressed intercept. Thus, when values for both independent

---

[6] For every observation in the series (1947-1997), new variables were created. These variables represented consecutive lags for the installed platforms. For example, lag_1 for 1948 contains platforms installed in 1947; lag_2 for 1950 contains platforms installed in 1948, and so forth. In certain cases, statistical software created missing values. For example, lag_2 for 1948 is a missing value, because there were no platforms installed in 1946. All missing values were substituted with zeroes. Then, a step-wise OLS regression were performed with the annual number of removed platforms as a dependent variable and 40 lags (lag_1, lag_2,..., lag_40) of installed platforms as independent variables. Out of the 40 independent variables, the step-wise regression procedure selected, based on the resulting R square, ten best models. The first model included only one independent variable, the second model included two independent variables, and so forth up to ten. The model with two explanatory variables provided a much better fit than the model with just a single explanatory variable; however, a model with three explanatory variables provided only a marginal improvement over the model with two explanatory variables. Therefore, the model with the two lags–lag_32 and lag_21– was selected as the most parsimonious.

24

variables are set to zero, the value for the dependent variable is also equal to zero. The final relationships estimated in the equation state that 95.3 percent and 35.1 percent of platforms installed in year (t-33) and (t-21), respectively, are removed in year t.

The above estimated removal equation is obtained using statistical method that lacks the conceptual foundation that the forecasting equation for platform installations enjoys. But, the model explains more than 95 percent of the observed variation in platform removal. Parameter estimates of the independent variables are also statistically significant. However, the mean absolute percent error and the root mean square percent error of the predicted values are a high 22 and 21 percent, respectively. Figure 3.2 plots the actual and predicted number of removed platforms for the period 1947 - 1997.

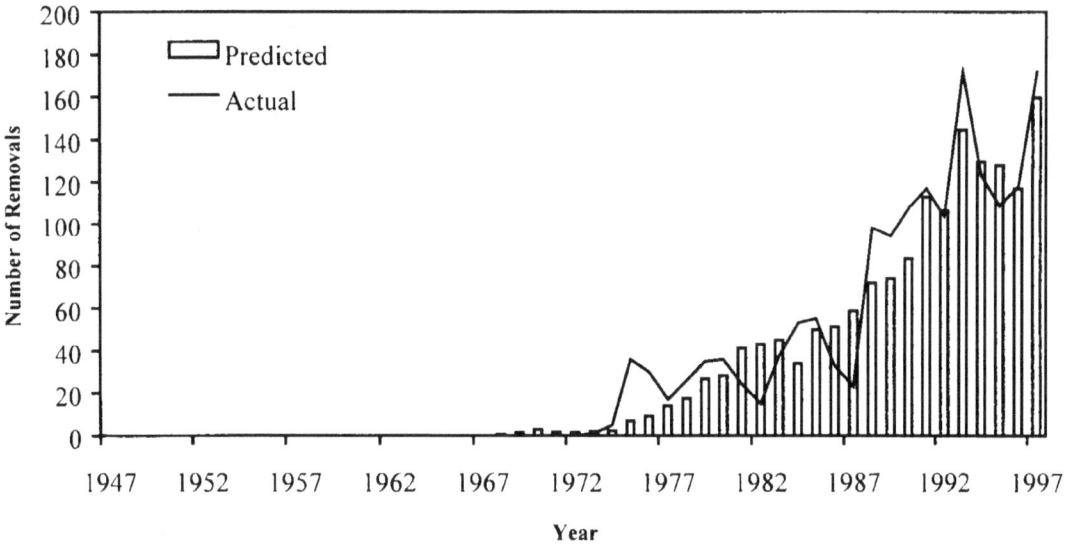

Figure 3.2. Actual and predicted number of platform removals.

3.4 Predicting Operating Platforms

By using equations (3-6) and (3-7) in combination with the identity equation (3-1), predicted values of operating platforms can be calculated. Figure 3.3 shows a pictorial view of the predicted number of operating platforms over the period for which we have data. The predicted values tracked the actual values quite well, with the moving average percent error (MAPE) for the period 1947-1997 being 7.75 percent while the root mean square is approximately 4.48 percent.

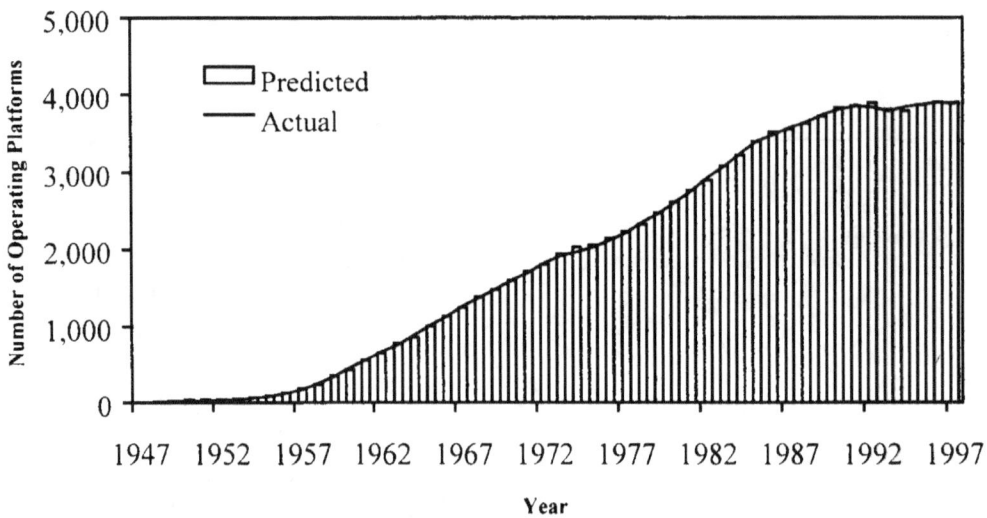

Figure 3.3. Actual and predicted number of operating platforms.

4. FORECASTING THE NUMBER OF OPERATING PLATFORMS

The model results presented in Table 3.1 were used to generate annual forecasts of the number of platforms installed for the period 1999-2023. The values assumed for all the parameters and variables used to forecast platform installations are reported in Table A.1 in Appendix A. Equations (3-6) and (3-7) were subsequently applied to calculate future removals and installations, and the corresponding number of platforms operating annually was estimated using the identity equation (3-1). The forecasting results are presented in Tables 4.1 and 4.2, and pictorial views of the forecasting results are presented in Figures 4.1-4.4.

4.1 Model Variables

Forecasting the number of platforms that will be installed over the next 25 years requires a prediction of the number and size of the new fields that these platforms are intended to develop and produce.

4.1.1 Drilling and Discovery Models: The drilling sub-model assumes that firms are risk neutral. Therefore, they simply maximize profits adjusted to reflect the value of money over time. Prices of oil and gas are exogenously determined in international markets. Firms engaged in exploration and production activities wish to maximize the expected value of a drilling plan. This value is the expected profit to be realized from successful wells over their producing life. A successful well by definition is one that finds hydrocarbons in commercial quantities. Prices, costs, and the regulatory environment are uncertain, however, so that a plan made in one period may not make economic sense in succeeding periods. In the face of this uncertainty, it is appropriate to consider each period's drilling plan separately.

Thus the firm's objective is to maximize the discounted profits of drilling wells in period t:

$$\text{Max } [PROFIT(t)] = [NOP * SUCC(WILDT) * SIZE(WILDT) * WELLS] \quad (4-1)$$

where:

  NOP = the net operating profit (wellhead price less taxes, royalty payments, and operating costs);
  SUCC = the probability that a well will be successful and is a declining function of the total number of wildcat wells drilled in the Gulf of Mexico OCS to date;
  WILDT = total number of wild cat wells drilled in the Gulf of Mexico OCS;
  SIZE = the expected size of new discoveries resulting from drilling undertaken in the period and is a declining function of the total number of wildcat wells drilled in the Gulf of Mexico OCS to date;
  WELLS = the number of new wildcat wells drilled in the period.

Reflecting the nature of the exploratory process, the probability of success and the expected size of new discoveries are declining functions of the total number of wildcat wells drilled in a region. In addition, the expected size of new discoveries, *i.e.*, the volume of recoverable hydrocarbons in a formation, is positively related to the probability of discovery. This echos the

27

familiar precept that the largest fields in a region tend to be found first, with smaller fields discovered later (Arps and Roberts, 1958, and Attanasi and Haynes, 1983).

Maximizing equation (4-1) with respect to WELLS yields a drilling plan:

$$WELLS^* = fn(NOP, SUCC, SIZE, NTLL) = fn(NOP, NTLL, WILDT) \qquad (4-2)$$

where:
> WELLS* = optimal number of new wild cat wells drilled;
> NTLL = number of tracts leased in the previous period.

This is called the drilling model and can be made operational by recursively predicting the next period's drilling activity from the previous period's cumulative wild cat wells drilled, discovery size, and discovery probability, *i.e.*, the success rate from the previous period's drilling. Firms operating in the Gulf of Mexico are not entirely free to drill anywhere, however, so the number of tracts leased in the previous period is also included in the model. This is also assumed to be exogenous in each lease sale.

Following Arps and Roberts (1958), it is assumed that for any given size class of field, the probability of field discovery is directly proportional to the number of undiscovered fields remaining in that class in the region and to the ratio of the average surface area of fields in that class to the overall area of the region. Attanasi and Haynes (1983) achieved good predictive results for estimating the number of undiscovered fields remaining in a size class by using the following analytical form as an estimating equation for fields (the discovery model):

$$F_i(WILDT) = F_i(\infty)(1-EXP(-(C_i.A_i.WELLS)/B)) \qquad (4-3)$$

where:
> $F_i(WILDT)$ = the cumulative number of fields in size class i expected to have been discovered after drilling WILDT exploratory wells;
> $F_i(\infty)$ = the ultimate (unknown) number of fields in size class i;
> B = the area of the region;
> A = the average area of the fields in size class i;
> C_i = a parameter representing the efficiency of discovery of fields in size class i;
> $F_i(\infty)$ and C_i are parameters to be estimated using observations on the other variables.

There is a factor that complicates the implementation of equation (4-3). Generally, only those fields large enough to be economically viable are reported. Smaller fields may have been found but not reported, hence they would not be included in the data used to estimate equation (4-3). Attanasi and Haynes referred to this problem as economic truncation and noted that it could cause biased estimates of $F_i(\infty)$ and C_i for those size classes in which economic truncation occurs.

The work of Drew, et al. (1982) is useful in addressing this problem. Based on observations of highly developed regions, they proposed that field sizes are distributed log-normally. They determined the largest size class which exhibits economic truncation as the class for which

28

discovery rates did not significantly decline with time in the study region. They use as the estimate of Fi(∞) for that size class the estimated ultimate number of fields of the next larger size class, Fi(∞), multiplied by 1.65 (Drew, et al., 1982, pp. 17-22).

For size classes that exhibit economic truncation, it is only necessary to estimate the efficiency of discovery Ci after calculating Fi(∞) using the economic truncation factor. Drew, et al. used a factor of 1.65 based on observations of size classes that do not exhibit economic truncation; a different factor could be used, of course, according to the region being studied. We used the same factor, since Drew, et al. calculated this factor based on a study of the Western Gulf of Mexico and because it is slightly lower than the calculated factor for the data in this study (1.72) and therefore a little more conservative.

4.1.2 Drilling and Discovery Results: The discovery model can be used in conjunction with the drilling model to recursively generate drilling and discovery forecasts. To illustrate, using 1996 data on the number and size of new discoveries and the number of wildcat wells drilled, an average size of discovery and a success rate can be calculated. These values can be used as SIZE and SUCC, respectively, in the drilling model to estimate the number of wildcat wells drilled in 1997. The forecast number of wildcat wells drilled can then be used in the discovery model to calculate new values for Fi(WILDT). This process can be carried out to estimate future drilling activity and discoveries under any number of scenarios by varying the future net operating profit assumption and assumptions about the number of tracts leased each year.

The results of estimating the drilling model are reported in Table 4.1. This second-order auto-correlation model shows that drilling activity is positively and significantly related to all four explanatory variables (all variables have been lagged one year).

The results of estimating the discovery model are reported in Table 4.2. It appears, based on the work of Drew et al. that economic truncation begins at size class 11. Therefore, statistical estimation of the ultimate number of fields and discovery efficiencies was carried out for size classes 18 through 12 only. For the remaining size classes, the number of fields was estimated using the economic truncation factor outlined above.

29

Table 4.1

Drilling Model Results (t- statistic in parenthesis)

Variable	Coefficient
Intercept	-14.473
	(-0.74)
Size (SIZE)	0.3342
	(1.830)
Success Rate (SUCC)	236.80
	(3.940)
Number of Tracts Leased (NTL)	0.0812
	(6.920)
Net Operating Profit (NOP)	4.7866
	(5.740)

Observations	49
AIC	213.470
SBC	221.419

Table 4.2

Discovery Model Results

Class	Size Range (MMBOE) Upper	Lower	Known Fields	Estimated Total	C, (95% CI)
18	777.2	388.6	9	9	1.97 (0.1 - 6.4)
17	388.6	194.3	31	35	2.00 (0.3 - 3.7)
16	194.3	97.2	75	80	1.00 (0.6 - 1.4)
15	97.2	48.6	84	118	1.00 (0.6 - 1.4)
14	48.6	24.3	117	169	1.00 (0.6 - 1.4)
13	24.3	12.14	143	213	1.00 (0.5 - 1.5)
12	12.14	6.07	121	188	1.00 (0.1 - 2.2)
11*	6.07	3.04	127	200	1.00**
10	3.04	1.52	96	329	1.00
9	1.52	0.76	44	544	1.00
8	0.76	0.38	33	897	1.00
7	0.38	0.19	19	1480	1.00

* Truncation begins at Class 11
** lower bound

4.2 Forecasting Model Variables

4.2.1 New Fields: Forecasting results for the base case, assuming that NOP is constant and that the number of tracts leased is constant, are reported in Table 4.3. The results are consistent with *a priori* expectations that the average size of new discoveries will decline as drilling proceeds. The success rates may seem somewhat low, but this is a result of using data from 1970 to 1993. Higher success rates are a relatively recent phenomenon, thus are not heavily weighted in the data.[7] The drilling and discovery sub-models yield estimates of new fields rather than our objective, new platforms.

4.2.2 Wellhead Price: The U.S. Department of Energy's Energy Information Administration (EIA) forecasts wellhead prices for crude oil in the lower 48 states under three scenarios: reference, high, and low prices (Annual Energy Outlook,1997, p 57). Based on EIA's forecasts of a declining (but positive) growth rate for both oil prices and economic growth (AEO, 1997, p 76), the reference price growth rates we calculated for the periods 2000-2005, 2006-2010, and 2011-2023 are 1.34%, 0.69%, and 0.55%, respectively.

To capture the uncertainties in the oil prices so as to examine the price impact on the number of operating platforms correspondingly, we used EIA's projection of high and low prices to calculate the high and low boundaries of expected prices. This is done in a similar manner to the method used to calculate the variations for new field size, *i.e.*, take the standard error of the EIA low price forecast and subtract two standard errors from the low forecast and add two standard errors to the high price forecast.

4.3 Operating Platform Forecasts and Analysis

4.3.1 The Reference Case Forecast: The reference forecast, or the forecast that in our view is the most likely, is summarized in Table 4.4.

During the forecast period the forecast calls for new platforms to be installed at an annual rate of about 142 platforms per year. Over the 25-year period, 3,543 platforms would be installed. Figure 4.1 illustrates the installation forecast and compares it to the historical record.

The number of platforms forecast to be removed is illustrated in Figure 4.2. A total of 4,645 platforms are forecast to be removed, which is an approximate annual rate of about 186 over the forecast period.

The number of platforms forecast to be operating in each year is shown in Figure 4.3. Operating platforms are predicted to decrease in number from 3,687 in 1999 to 2,612 in the year 2023. This is a decline of 1,075 or about 29 percent.

---

[7] The consequences of higher success rates are discussed in the following section.

Table 4.3

Base Case Forecasts of Wildcats, New Fields, Field Size, and Success Rate

Year	Wildcat Wells	New Fields	Field Size	Success Rate
1998	110	18	24.5	0.16
1999	114	14	15.4	0.11
2000	101	14	13.1	0.14
2001	104	12	16.9	0.12
2002	100	12	21.0	0.12
2003	103	13	34.8	0.13
2004	109	14	12.4	0.13
2005	102	11	17.6	0.11
2006	99	12	14.2	0.10
2007	101	10	15.2	0.10
2008	96	11	21.7	0.11
2009	102	11	14.6	0.11
2010	98	10	14.8	0.10
2011	96	10	38.4	0.10
2012	105	11	13.9	0.11
2013	97	8	9.3	0.08
2014	90	10	14.8	0.11
2015	98	7	5.4	0.07
2016	86	9	16.2	0.10
2017	97	9	8.8	0.09
2018	92	9	16.4	0.10
2019	96	8	4.9	0.08
2020	89	9	16.2	0.10
2021	97	8	9.3	0.08
2022	90	6	1.8	0.07
2023	84	9	32.3	0.11

Table 4.4

Reference Case Forecasts of the Number of Platforms to be Installed, Removed, and Operated on the Gulf of Mexico OCS, 1999 - 2023

Year	Platforms Operating	Platforms Installed	Platforms Removed
1999	3,687	137	165
2000	3,642	138	183
2001	3,623	138	158
2002	3,605	139	157
2003	3,566	140	178
2004	3,550	140	157
2005	3,498	141	193
2006	3,475	141	165
2007	3,529	142	87
2008	3,534	142	136
2009	3,510	142	166
2010	3,475	142	177
2011	3,402	142	215
2012	3,342	143	203
2013	3,292	143	192
2014	3,233	143	202
2015	3,130	143	246
2016	3,064	143	208
2017	2,957	143	251
2018	2,855	143	245
2019	2,849	143	149
2020	2,834	143	158
2021	2,772	144	206
2022	2,682	144	234
2023	2,612	144	214

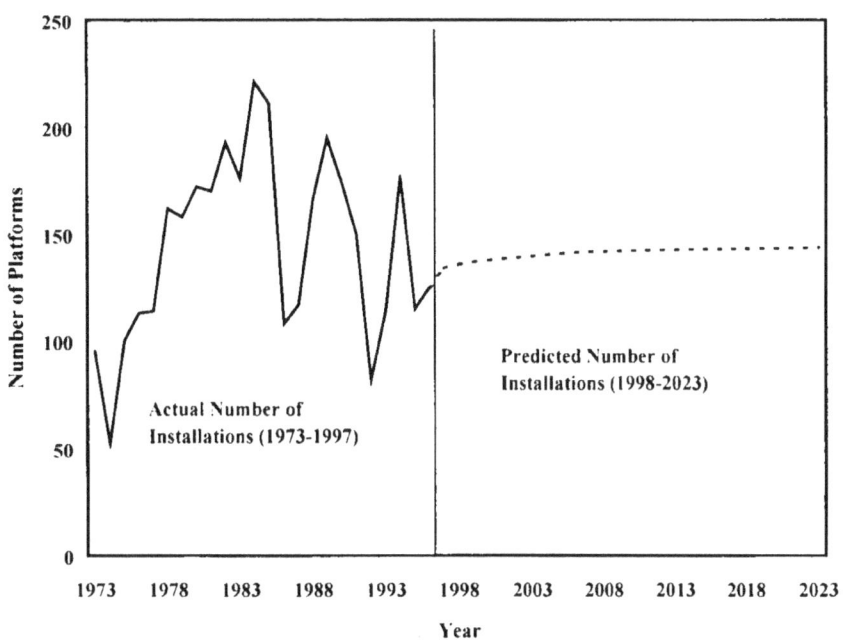

Figure 4.1. Actual and predicted platform installations.

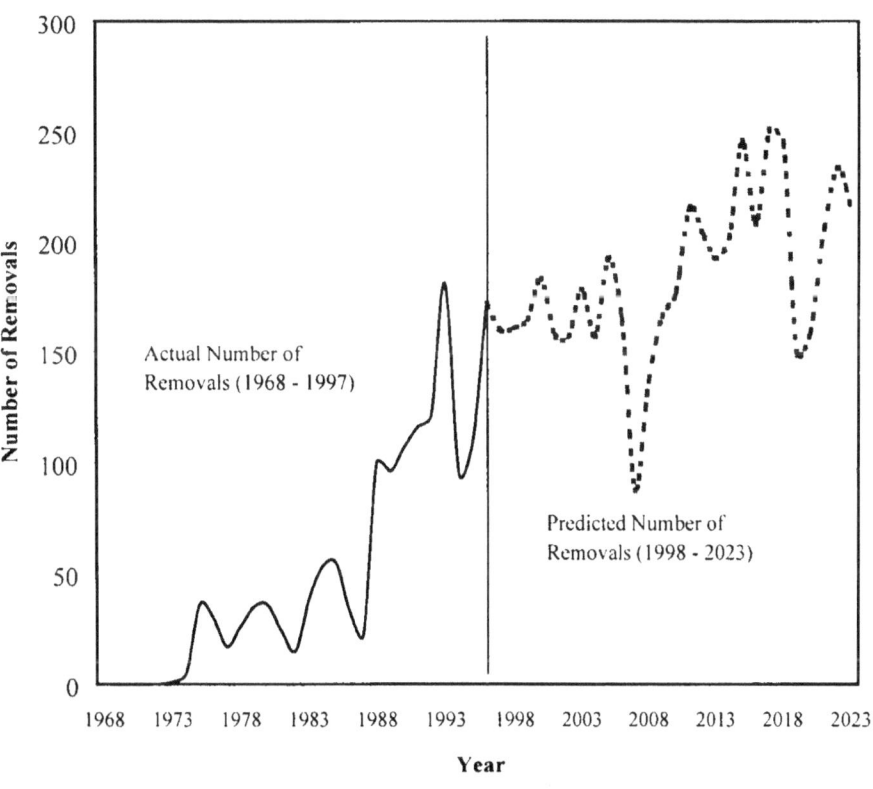

Figure 4.2. Actual and predicted platform removals.

35

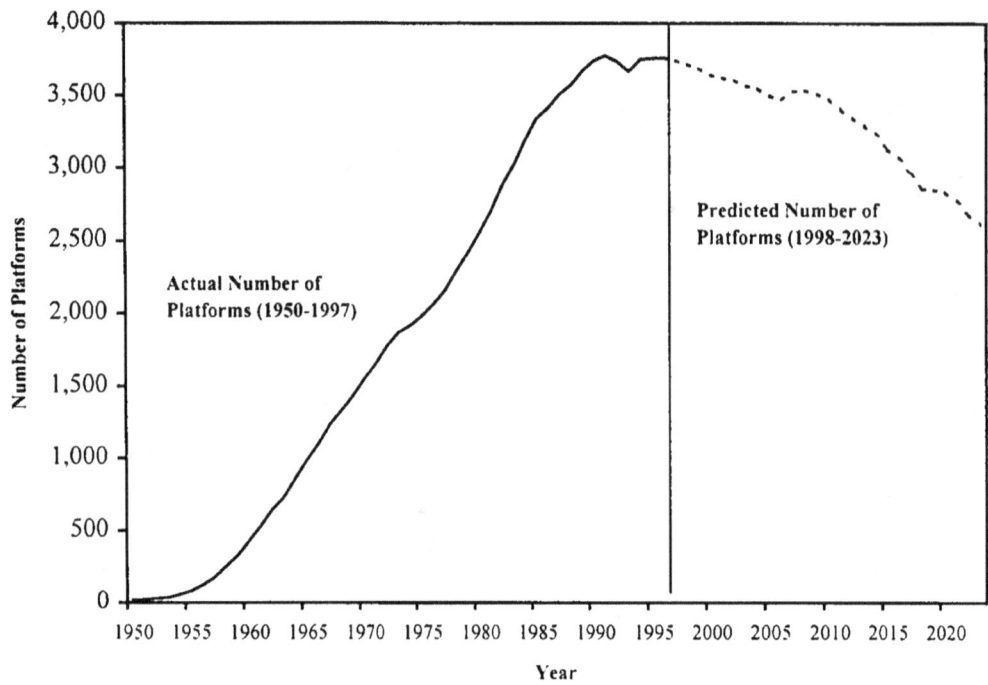

Figure 4.3. Platforms operating on the Gulf of Mexico OCS.

4.3.2 Sensitivity of the Forecast to Changes in Independent Variable: Table 4.5 compares four forecasts using differences in the number of operating platforms in the year 2023 relative to 1999 values and the reference forecast as measures. Tables giving year by year data for each forecast for the number of operating platforms, the number of platforms installed, and the number of platforms removed are shown in Appendix A.

The number of platforms operating in the high/low oil price forecast and the high/low new fields forecast is not very different from the values given in the reference forecast. This may seem somewhat surprising given the "impact" of low oil prices asserted by the oil and gas industry when prices decline. But offshore platforms are investments with a typical productive life of 10 to 20 or more years.

The decision to invest in a platform is not made based on the current price but on a range of expected future prices. Higher prices increase the return from the investment, but in the Gulf most platform investment decisions are undertaken with the expectation that the owners will at least recover their initial investment even at prices below $10/BOE. Platform installations may be postponed in low price periods because cash flow has slowed or stopped, external capital is too expensive, or other investments promise better returns; but most offshore platforms will continue to operate as long as returns exceed variable cost.

36

Table 4.5

Summary of Differences Among Reference and Alternative Forecasts 1999-2023

	FORECAST ASSUMPTIONS			
	Reference	EIA High & Low Prices	High New Field*	EIA & New Field Plus**
Platforms in 2023--High	18.91	16.15	15.96	15.76
Percent > Reference 2023	19.48	16.72	16.39	16.05
2023 as percent of 1999	20.38	17.62	17.05	16.51
Platforms in 2023--Low	21.12	18.36	17.64	16.92
Percent > Reference 2023	21.55	18.80	17.99	17.16
2023 as Percent of 1999	21.70	18.94	18.09	17.22

Source: See Appendix A. *High New Field is New Field plus 2 Std. Errors. **EIA and New Field Plus is EIA high price plus 2 Std. Errors and New field plus 2 std. errors. Note: Std. Errors are deviations in EIA and Field forecasts.

Conversely, high prices are unlikely to result in a major acceleration in installations of platforms. Over the past thirty years operators have repeatedly seen high prices erode as low cost producers increase production from already developed fields. Similarly, they have seen costs of installing platforms rise as day rates for drilling platforms and ships are bid up. They have learned to expect prices to increase and decrease over a cycle and are unlikely to make major changes in investment plans because of short-term price fluctuations.

As Table 4.5 shows, substituting the high new field discovery series for the reference forecast of new fields would increase the number of operating platforms in the year 2023 by 66 and reduce the decline in the number of operating platforms over the 2000 to 2023 time period from 28 percent in the reference forecast to a little less than 26 percent. The low forecast of new fields would decrease the number of platforms operating by 48 and increase the percentage drop over the time period to 29.5 percent.

Using EIA's high or low forecasts of oil prices, rather than its reference forecast, results in similar, marginal changes in the platform forecast. Comparing in the year 1999 and the year 2023, the high EIA price forecast would increase the number of platforms operating in 2023 by 60 platforms over the reference forecast. The low price forecast would predict 91 fewer operating platforms. The decline in operating platforms would be about 26 percent in EIA's high price scenario and about 30 percent in low price case–compared to a decline of 28 percent in the reference case. Figure 4.4 shows the effects of adding two standard errors to EIA's oil price forecasts. Figure 4.5 illustrates the effects of the change on the platform forecast.

The third alternative case summarized in Table 4.4 is one in which both the oil price forecasts and the new field forecast are increased by two standard errors in the high cases and decreased by two standard errors in the low cases. In simpler terms, this means the price forecast was increased enough that statisticians would be confident that ninety-five percent of the time the actual price would be below (in the high price case) or above (in the low price case) the corresponding EIA price.

Under these assumptions, the number of operating platforms in the year 2023 is about 12.5 percent higher than the reference forecast and about 10 percent lower in the low price case. The decline in the number of operating platforms over the 2000 to 2020 period is slightly less than 20 percent in the high price case and 35 percent in the low price case compared to the 28 percent drop in the reference forecast.

Figure 4.6 compares the effects of the change to the reference forecast. The year-by-year forecasts for each of the alternatives summarized in Table 4.4–giving platforms installed, operating, and removed–are in Appendix A. Also included in the appendix is a table giving the oil prices assumed in the reference and alternative forecasts.

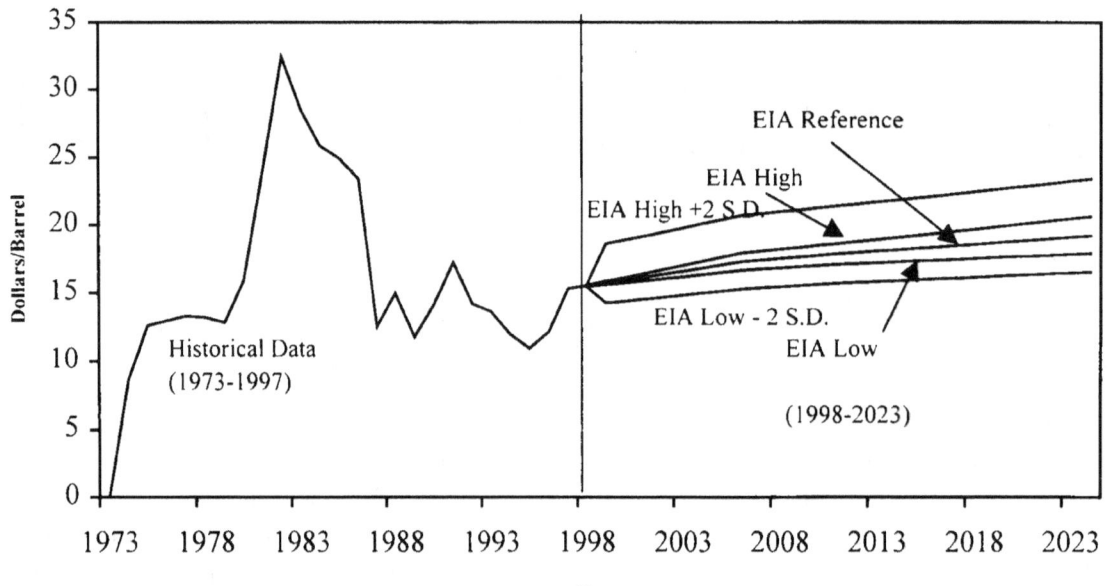

Figure 4.4. Predicted prices relative to EIA reference price.

38

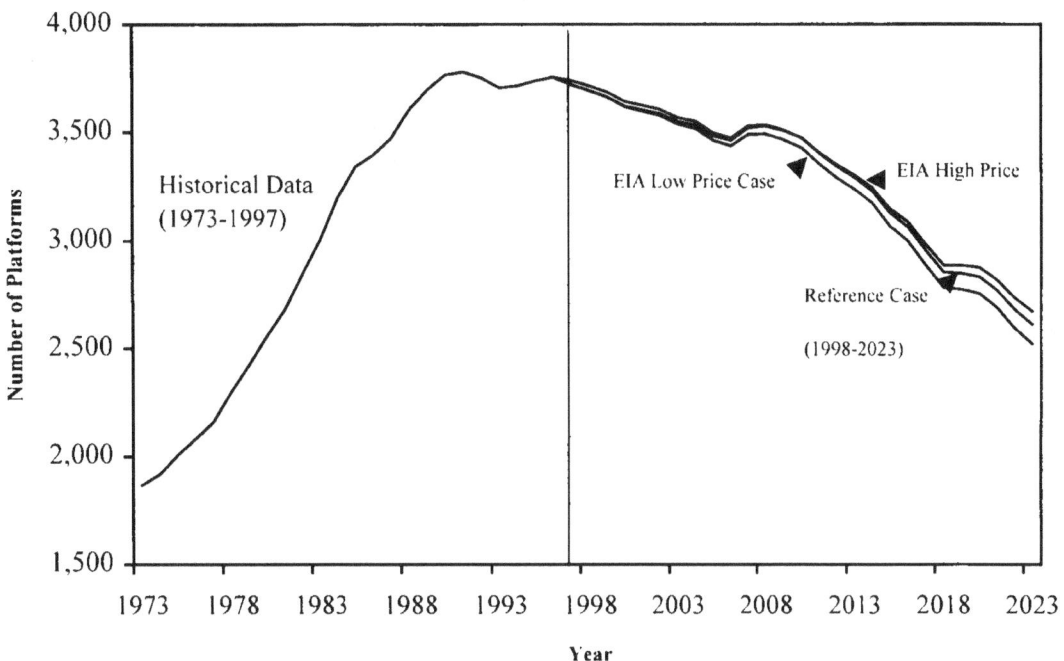

Figure 4.5. Predicted platforms using EIA price forecasts.

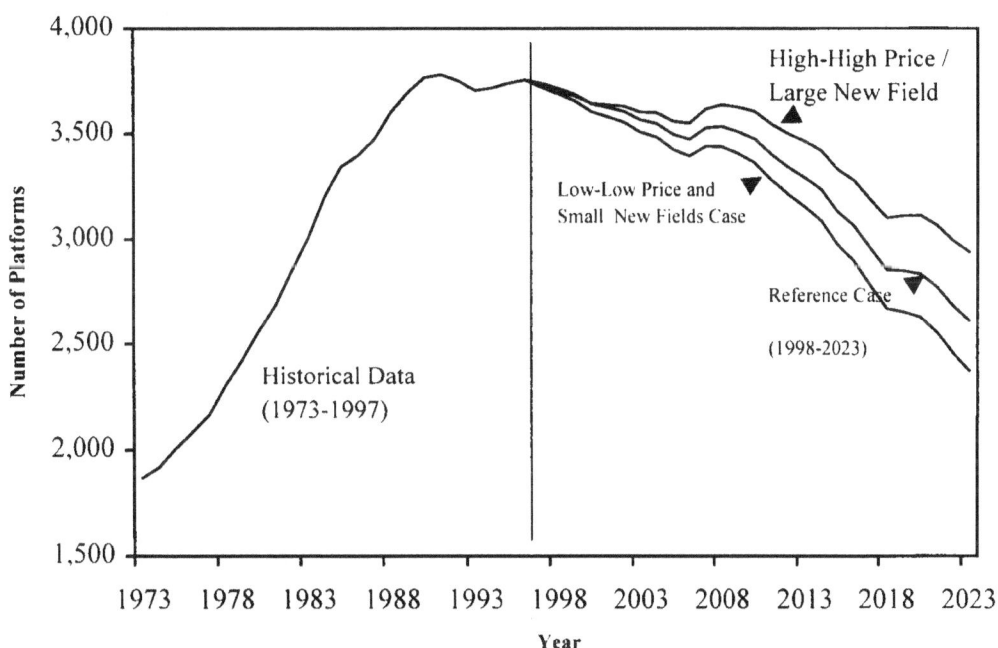

Figure 4.6. Operating platforms: alternative forecasts.

39

5. SUMMARY AND CONCLUSIONS

The total number of oil and gas platforms located in the federal or OCS part of the U.S. Gulf of Mexico is forecast to begin a slow but steady decline over the first quarter of the next century. The plateau of about 3,600 structures that was reached and maintained during the 1990s is a peak, according to the forecast, and the drop-off-period for the decline.

By the year 2023 the number of platforms in the Gulf is forecast to be roughly 2,600, a drop of 1,075 platforms for a total that will be about 29 percent below the current peak. Alternative forecasts made by changing the values of the forecasting variables did not result in major differences from the reference forecast. Even spreading the range of the values used in the forecasting equations by adding two standard errors to forecasting variables did not reverse the trends in the reference forecast. Adding or subtracting two standard errors to the cumulative size of new oil and gas field developed in the Gulf and to the Energy Information Agency's forecast of oil prices resulted in forecasts in which the decline in operating platforms in high forecast was still more than 20 percent, as compared to 29 percent in the reference forecast. The decline in the corresponding low forecast was about 35 percent.

According to the reference forecast– the following predictions can be made:

- The number of platforms operating in the Gulf will decline as the result of an increase in the annual number of platforms removed over historical levels while the number of new platforms installed each year will increase very slowly. This is the reverse of the historic pattern in which removals have usually fallen short of installations, producing an increase in the number of operating platforms.

- The number of platforms installed annually will increase from an estimated 138 in the year 2000 to 144 in the year 2023, which is not much different than the average over the 1990s. The number of platforms annually removed from the Gulf OCS will move more irregularly than installations, varying from a low of 87 in 2007 to a high of 246 in the year 2015. These annual numbers are given only to indicate range our methods and objectives are designed to forecast longer-term trends, not precise, yearly magnitudes or changes. A principal reason for the variation is that the removal forecast is driven by the number of installations in previous years. As the forecast encounters unusually high or low numbers of historical installations, the removal estimate changes accordingly. The forecasts of installations and removals were made separately with different methods.

- Installations were estimated using an econometric model driven by estimates of the rate of discovery of new petroleum fields and the size of those fields, technological trends in petroleum exploration and production, prices for crude oil, and the shock of the oil price collapse in the mid-1980s. The estimating equation had the "correct" signs , *i.e.*, was consistent with our hypotheses and explained about 79 percent of the variation in platform installations.

41

- Platform removals were estimated with a purely statistical approach that measured the association between the number of platforms removed and the number of platforms installed in each previous year. Doing this interactively for each year's (1947 to 1997) removals and all preceding year's installations enabled us to pick the number of years (referred to as "lags") in which the number of installations is most closely associated with the number of removals so many years in the future. The best model from a forecasting viewpoint predicted removals based on the number of platforms installed, or lags, of 32 and 21 years in the past. The estimating equation for platform removals explained about 95.2 percent of the variation in the historical data on removed platforms.

The reference forecast, despite its hybrid ancestry, fits fairly well with current industry trends and opinion, although longer term forecasting is not a topic to which the industry has paid much attention. Nevertheless, a common industry view is that as exploration and production move into the deep (and deeper) Gulf, larger and more complex platforms will be installed. This, when coupled with advanced seismic imaging and directional drilling, means that more wells can be drilled from a single platform. On the other side, these same factors also make feasible the production of smaller fields in shallow and intermediate depth waters with smaller, simpler and frequently re-used platforms. Indeed, as discussed earlier, although about 80 percent of the approximately 1,500 platforms removed from the Gulf were non-major structures (major structures having at least six completed wells and two pieces production equipment) about 25 percent of the smaller, non-major structures were less than five years old. But the net result, in our view, is that shown in the reference forecast– a slow but steady decline in the number of platforms operating in the federal OCS Gulf of Mexico.

A slow and steady decline in the number of platforms does not necessarily imply a decline in oil and gas production or less economic activity related to the development of the offshore. Indeed, production per platform has increased since the early 1990s. As more and more production comes from the very large deep Gulf wells, we expect this trend to continue. Similarly, with the number of installations increasing, albeit very slowly, and expenditures to install each platform increasing as the proportion of larger platforms located in deeper waters grows coupled with a significant increase in the number of platforms removed, economic activity associated with offshore oil and gas exploration and production is likely to increase.

6. REFERENCES

Arps, J.J. and T.G. Roberts. 1958. "Economics of Drilling for Cretaceous Oil on East Flank of Denver-Julesburg Basin," Bulletin of the American Association of Petroleum Geologists, 42 (11), November.

Attanasi, E.D. and J.L. Haynes. 1983. "Future Supply of Oil and Gas from the Gulf of Mexico." U. S. Geological Survey Professional Paper #1294.

Bohi, D.R. 1997. *Changing Productivity of Petroleum Exploration and Development in the U.S.* Resources for the Future Discussion Paper, January 1997, Washington D.C.

Drew, L.J., J.H. Schuenmeyer, and W.J. Bawiec. 1982. "Estimation of the Future Rates of Oil and Gas Discoveries in the Western Gulf of Mexico," U.S. Geological Survey Professional Paper #1252.

Energy Information Administration. 1997. *Annual Energy Outlook 1997 with projections to 2015*, DOE/EIA-0383(97).

Iledare, O.O., A.G. Pulsipher, and R.H. Baumann. 1995. "Effects of an Increasing Role for Independents on Petroleum Resource Development in the Gulf of Mexico OCS Region." *The Energy Journal.* 16(2):59-76.

Kennedy, P. 1992. *An Guide to Econometrics*, 3rd edition. The MIT Press, Cambridge, Massachusetts.

Marine Board. 1985. Committee on Disposition of Offshore Platforms, Marine Board National Research Council, Disposal of Offshore Platforms, National Academy Press.

APPENDIX A - FORECASTING VARIABLES AND MODEL RESULTS

Table A.1
Estimated Values of Model Variables and Parameters Used to Forecast the Number of Platforms Installed
from 1998-2023

Year	Wildcats Wells	New Fields #	Field Size (MMBOE)*	Success Rate	Avg. Well Head Price (Dollars/Bbl)
1998	110	18	24.5	0.16	15.74
1999	114	14	15.4	0.12	15.96
2000	101	14	13.1	0.14	16.17
2001	104	12	16.9	0.12	16.38
2002	100	12	21.0	0.12	16.61
2003	103	13	34.8	0.13	16.83
2004	109	14	12.4	0.13	17.05
2005	102	11	17.6	0.11	17.28
2006	99	12	14.2	0.12	17.40
2007	101	10	15.2	0.10	17.52
2008	96	11	21.7	0.11	17.64
2009	102	11	14.6	0.11	17.77
2010	98	10	14.8	0.10	17.89
2011	96	10	38.4	0.10	17.99
2012	105	11	13.9	0.11	18.06
2013	97	8	9.3	0.08	18.19
2014	90	10	14.8	0.11	18.29
2015	98	7	5.4	0.07	18.39
2016	86	9	16.2	0.10	18.49
2017	97	9	8.8	0.09	18.59
2018	92	9	16.4	0.10	18.69
2019	96	8	4.9	0.08	18.80
2020	89	9	16.2	0.10	18.90
2021	97	8	9.3	0.08	19.00
2022	90	6	1.8	0.07	19.11
2023	84	9	32.3	0.11	19.22

* Million Barrels of Oil Equivalent

Table A.2
Crude Oil Price Forecasts. EIA's High, Low, and Reference Forecast; EIA's High Plus Two Standard Errors (High-Plus); and EIA's Low Forecasts Minus Two Standard Errors (Low Minus) for the 1999 - 2023 Period

Year	High Plus	EIA High	EIA Reference	EIA Low	Low Minus
1999	18.91	16.15	15.96	15.76	14.41
2000	19.19	16.43	16.17	15.91	14.55
2001	19.48	16.72	16.39	16.05	14.70
2002	19.77	17.02	16.61	16.20	14.85
2003	20.07	17.32	16.83	16.35	15.00
2004	20.38	17.62	17.05	16.51	15.15
2005	20.69	17.93	17.28	16.66	15.30
2006	20.83	18.07	17.40	16.75	15.39
2007	20.97	18.21	17.52	16.83	15.48
2008	21.12	18.36	17.64	16.92	15.57
2009	21.26	18.51	17.77	17.01	15.66
2010	21.41	18.65	17.89	17.10	15.74
2011	21.55	18.80	17.99	17.16	15.81
2012	21.70	18.94	18.09	17.22	15.87
2013	21.85	19.09	18.19	17.28	15.93
2014	21.99	19.24	18.29	17.34	15.99
2015	22.14	19.39	18.39	17.41	16.05
2016	22.29	19.54	18.49	17.47	16.11
2017	22.44	19.69	18.59	17.53	16.18
2018	22.60	19.84	18.69	17.59	16.24
2019	22.75	19.99	18.80	17.66	16.30
2020	22.90	20.15	18.90	17.72	16.37
2021	23.06	20.30	19.01	17.78	16.43
2022	23.22	20.46	19.11	17.85	16.49
2023	23.28	20.62	19.22	17.91	16.56

Note: Std. Errors are deviations in EIA forecasts.

Table A.3
Predicted Number of Platforms to be Installed, Removed, and Operated on the Gulf of Mexico OCS Under Three U.S. DOE/EIA Price Projections*, 1999 - 2023

Year	Operating Platforms			Installations			Removals
	Case I	Case II	Case III	Case I	Case II	Case III	
1999	3,665	3,687	3,663	136	137	135	165
2000	3,620	3,642	3,616	138	138	136	183
2001	3,601	3,623	3,596	139	138	137	158
2002	3,585	3,605	3,576	140	139	138	157
2003	3,548	3,566	3,536	141	140	138	178
2004	3,533	3,550	3,518	142	140	139	157
2005	3,484	3,498	3,464	143	141	139	193
2006	3,463	3,475	3,439	144	141	139	165
2007	3,520	3,529	3,490	144	142	139	87
2008	3,528	3,534	3,493	145	142	139	136
2009	3,508	3,510	3,467	145	142	139	166
2010	3,476	3,475	3,430	145	142	140	177
2011	3,406	3,402	3,354	146	142	140	215
2012	3,349	3,342	3,290	146	143	140	203
2013	3,303	3,292	3,238	146	143	140	192
2014	3,248	3,233	3,175	147	143	140	202
2015	3,149	3,130	3,069	147	143	140	246
2016	3,088	3,064	3,000	147	143	140	208
2017	3,985	2,957	2,889	148	143	140	251
2018	2,887	2,855	2,784	148	143	140	245
2019	2,887	2,849	2,774	148	143	140	149
2020	2,877	2,834	2,755	149	143	140	158
2021	2,821	2,772	2,689	149	144	140	206
2022	2,736	2,682	2,595	149	144	140	234
2023	2,672	2,612	2,521	150	144	140	214

* Case I: EIA high prices; Case II: Reference prices; Case III: EIA low prices.

Table A.4
Predicted Number of Platforms to be Installed, Removed and Operated on the Gulf of Mexico OCS with EIA High Price Plus Two Standard Errors and EIA Low Minus Two Standard Errors, 1999 - 2023

Year	Operated Platforms			Installations			Removals
	Case I	Case II	Case III	Case I	Case II	Case III	
1999	3,679	3,687	3,656	144	137	131	165
2000	3,643	3,642	3,604	148	138	132	183
2001	3,635	3,623	3,579	149	138	132	158
2002	3,629	3,605	3,554	151	139	133	157
2003	3,603	3,566	3,509	152	140	133	178
2004	3,598	3,550	3,485	153	140	133	157
2005	3,559	3,498	3,426	154	141	134	193
2006	3,549	3,475	3,395	154	141	134	165
2007	3,617	3,529	3,442	155	142	134	87
2008	3,635	3,534	3,439	155	142	134	136
2009	3,624	3,510	3,407	155	142	134	166
2010	3,603	3,475	3,364	156	142	134	177
2011	3,544	3,402	3,283	156	142	134	215
2012	3,497	3,342	3,214	156	143	134	203
2013	3,461	3,292	3,156	157	143	134	192
2014	3,416	3,233	3,088	157	143	134	202
2015	3,327	3,130	2,976	157	143	134	246
2016	3,276	3,064	2,902	157	143	134	208
2017	3,183	2,957	2,784	158	143	134	251
2018	3,096	2,855	2,673	158	143	134	245
2019	3,106	2,849	2,658	158	143	134	149
2020	3,106	2,834	2,634	159	143	134	158
2021	3,059	2,772	2,562	159	144	134	206
2022	2,985	2,682	2,462	159	144	134	234
2023	2,931	2,612	2,382	160	144	134	214

Note: Case I: EIA high prices plus two standard errors; Case II: Reference prices; Case III: EIA low prices minus two standard errors.

Table A.5
Alternative Forecasts of High(Case I), Low (Case III), and Reference (Case II) Forecasts of New Field Discoveries and the Reference Price Forecast

Year	Platforms To Be Operated			Platforms To Be Installed			Platforms To Be Removed
	Case I	Case II	Case III	Case I	Case II	Case III	
1999	3,690	3,687	3,680	136	137	135	165
2000	3,644	3,642	3,634	137	138	137	183
2001	3,624	3,623	3,615	138	138	138	158
2002	3,607	3,605	3,598	139	139	139	157
2003	3,569	3,566	3,559	140	140	140	178
2004	3,552	3,550	3,542	140	140	141	157
2005	3,501	3,498	3,490	141	141	141	193
2006	3,477	3,475	3,467	141	141	141	165
2007	3,532	3,529	3,521	142	142	142	87
2008	3,539	3,534	3,526	142	142	142	136
2009	3,516	3,510	3,502	143	142	142	166
2010	3,482	3,475	3,467	143	142	142	177
2011	3,410	3,402	3,393	143	142	142	215
2012	3,351	3,342	3,332	143	143	142	203
2013	3,302	3,292	3,282	143	143	142	192
2014	3,244	3,233	3,223	143	143	142	202
2015	3,141	3,130	3,119	143	143	142	246
2016	3,076	3,064	3,053	143	143	143	208
2017	2,969	2,957	2,945	144	143	143	251
2018	2,868	2,855	2,843	144	143	143	245
2019	2,864	2,849	2,837	144	143	143	149
2020	2,850	2,834	2,821	144	143	143	158
2021	2,788	2,772	2,759	144	144	143	206
2022	2,698	2,682	2,668	144	144	143	234
2023	2,628	2,612	2,598	144	144	143	214

Note: Case I: Reference new fields plus two standard errors;   Case II: Reference new fields; Case III: Reference new fields minus two standard errors.
Prices are kept at the reference case.

Table A.6
Predicted Number of Platforms to be Installed, Removed, and Operated with Both Price and New Fields Increased by Two Standard Errors (Case I) and Both Variables Decreased by Two Standard Errors (Case III) on the Gulf of Mexico OCS, 1999 - 2023

Year	Platforms To Be Operated			Platforms To Be Installed			Platforms To Be Removed
	Case I	Case II	Case III	Case I	Case II	Case III	
1999	3,679	3,687	3,656	144	137	131	165
2000	3,643	3,642	3,604	148	138	132	183
2001	3,635	3,623	3,579	149	138	132	158
2002	3,629	3,605	3,554	151	139	132	157
2003	3,603	3,566	3,509	152	140	133	178
2004	3,599	3,550	3,485	153	140	133	157
2005	3,560	3,498	3,425	154	141	133	193
2006	3,550	3,475	3,394	155	141	134	165
2007	3,617	3,529	3,441	155	142	134	87
2008	3,636	3,534	3,438	155	142	134	136
2009	3,626	3,510	3,406	156	142	134	166
2010	3,605	3,475	3,363	156	142	134	177
2011	3,546	3,402	3,281	156	142	134	215
2012	3,499	3,342	3,212	157	143	134	203
2013	3,464	3,292	3,153	157	143	134	192
2014	3,419	3,233	3,085	157	143	134	202
2015	3,331	3,130	2,972	158	143	134	246
2016	3,281	3,064	2,898	158	143	134	208
2017	3,188	2,957	2,780	158	143	133	251
2018	3,101	2,855	2,668	159	143	133	245
2019	3,111	2,849	2,653	159	143	133	149
2020	3,112	2,834	2,628	159	143	133	158
2021	3,066	2,772	2,556	160	144	133	206
2022	2,993	2,682	2,455	160	144	133	234
2023	2,939	2,612	2,374	160	144	133	214

Note: Case I: high prices and high new fields plus two standard errors; Case II: Reference prices and reference new fields; Case III: low prices and low new fields minus two standard errors .

52

The Department of the Interior Mission

As the Nation's principal conservation agency, the Department of the Interior has responsibility for most of our nationally owned public lands and natural resources. This includes fostering sound use of our land and water resources; protecting our fish, wildlife, and biological diversity; preserving the environmental and cultural values of our national parks and historical places; and providing for the enjoyment of life through outdoor recreation. The Department assesses our energy and mineral resources and works to ensure that their development is in the best interests of all our people by encouraging stewardship and citizen participation in their care. The Department also has a major responsibility for American Indian reservation communities and for people who live in island territories under U.S. administration.

The Minerals Management Service Mission

As a bureau of the Department of the Interior, the Minerals Management Service's (MMS) primary responsibilities are to manage the mineral resources located on the Nation's Outer Continental Shelf (OCS), collect revenue from the Federal OCS and onshore Federal and Indian lands, and distribute those revenues.

Moreover, in working to meet its responsibilities, the **Offshore Minerals Management Program** administers the OCS competitive leasing program and oversees the safe and environmentally sound exploration and production of our Nation's offshore natural gas, oil and other mineral resources. The MMS **Royalty Management Program** meets its responsibilities by ensuring the efficient, timely and accurate collection and disbursement of revenue from mineral leasing and production due to Indian tribes and allottees, States and the U.S. Treasury.

The MMS strives to fulfill its responsibilities through the general guiding principles of: (1) being responsive to the public's concerns and interests by maintaining a dialogue with all potentially affected parties and (2) carrying out its programs with an emphasis on working to enhance the quality of life for all Americans by lending MMS assistance and expertise to economic development and environmental protection.